I0694276

WHILE WE'RE HERE

China stories from a writers' colony

Edited by Alec Ash & Tom Pellman

While We're Here
China stories from a writers' colony

Edited by Alec Ash and Tom Pellman

ISBN-13: 978-988-82737-6-8

This book has been reset in 10pt Book Antiqua. Spellings and punctuations are left as in the original edition.

LCO000000 LITERARY/ COLLECTIONS/ General

EB074

Published by Earnshaw Books Ltd. (Hong Kong)

For our friends

Contents

Foreword   1

Jonathan Rechtman   Model Worker   5

Tom Pellman   The Tiger Suit   11

Sascha Matuszak   Flower Town   16

Anthony Tao   Writers in China   33

Karoline Kan   Examining the Past   35

Josh Stenberg   The View   41

David Moser   The Book of Changes   44

Tom Fearon   State of Media   56

Carlos Ottery   Big in Beijing   60

Sam Duncan   Ayi and I   64

Rosalyn Shih   Mid-Autumn Lanterns   73

Carl Setzer   The Cornfield Grave   74

Michael Salmon   Dumplings   78

Cobus Block   Life is an Internet Café   85

Canaan Morse   Nursery Rhyme for Beijing   91

Robert Foyle Hunwick   Shower Business   92

Alicia Lui   Censor   100

Laszlo Montgomery	Made in China	103
Jonathan Kos-Read	I'm Not a Communist, But I Play One on TV	108
Kaiser Kuo	Old Chokey Christmas	120
Peta Zhimin Rush	Family Footsteps	124
Magdalena Navarro	Short Nails, White Socks	129
Jesse Field	Awkward Lavender	138
Jeremiah Jenne	The Mountain Spirits are Laughing	141
Tom Mangione	Rice Fields	152
Aaron Fox-Lerner	Back and Forth	155
Mia Li	Over the Wall	166
Courtney Han	Roots and Leaves	171
Hannah Lincoln	Love, Anywhere	183
Brent Crane	Ramadan in Kashgar	189
Yuan Yang	Emei City	194
Alec Ash	In the Hutong	196
Daniel Tam-Claiborne	If Not for the Melon	206
Contributors		209
Notes		214

FOREWORD

WE ARE ALL writers, in the stories we tell about ourselves and the world around us. For those of us who came to China, everyone has a tale or ten to spin, whether it's at the bar or on a blog. It's hard not to when you live here. Some of those stories are familiar, others a surprise. Most are lost at the bottom of a cocktail, a few end up on the printed page.

To publish stories that would otherwise go untold was the founding philosophy of our "writers' colony" *the Anthill* (theanthill.org). In the autumn of 2012, there were plenty of China blogs that regurgitated the news, but precious few that posted personal narratives with a sense of story. Tom Pellman joined as fiction editor soon after, expanding the scope of the site to something altogether more literary, and Anthony Tao did the same with poetry. We accepted photography and translations as well, and found a loyal following.

Now, some three years later, there are over a hundred writers in the colony. (Our name comes from the Chinese phrase "ant tribe" that describes directionless college graduates; foreigner twentysomethings who wind up in China may recognize the clan.) We've hosted two storytelling events – "Writers and Rum" at Cuju, a Moroccan bistro and rum bar, and "Scotch and Stories" at the Beijing Bookworm – which were both sold out and *very* boozy. And now, thanks to our publisher Graham Earnshaw, we add the book you're holding in your hands.

While We're Here is an anthology (ant-ology?) of posts from *the*

Anthill's three years. It's a mix of narrative non-fiction – ever our core – and fiction, with a smattering of poetry for good measure. There are 33 contributions, some a single page, others twenty. Most of our writers, like many of our readers, are foreigners in China or ethnic Chinese who grew up overseas. All proceeds from the book will go to The Library Project (library-project. org), a charity that donates books to rural primary schools and orphanages in Asia – our small way of giving something back.

The anthology is designed to be dipped into rather than read cover-to-cover, but follows a loosely seasonal structure. We begin with Jonathan Rechtman's spring fling as a foreign model for a charismatic Frenchman ("Model Worker", p.5). Other summer exploits include Sascha Matuszak's wonderful long-form account of a Sichuanese village during the 2008 earthquake ("Flower Town", p.16), a cross-generational *gaokao* history by Karoline Kan ("Examining the Past", p. 35) and flash fiction by Josh Stenberg ("The View", p.41) before autumn falls.

In winter, Sam Duncan plunges us below zero degrees in Daqing, China's oil-rich far north ("Ayi and I", p.64), Carl Setzer pays last respects to his father in law ("The Cornfield Grave", p.74) and Robert Foyle Hunwick braves one of Beijing's last bathhouses ("Shower Business", p.92). Kaiser Kuo offers some festive verse for Christmas ("Old Chokey Christmas", p.120) and Peta Zhimin Rush reflects on her identity as half-British half-Chinese in time for Spring Festival ("Family Footsteps", p.124).

There are also fascinating personal reflections by contributors with decades in China under their belt, whether in China's jazz scene by David Moser ("The Book of Changes", p.44), in the manufacturing business by Laszlo Montgomery ("Made in China", p.103), or as a foreign actor by Jonathan Kos-Read ("I'm Not a Communist, But I Play One on TV", p.108). Then it's summer again, with Jeremiah Jenne's travels in Yunnan ("The

Mountain Spirits are Laughing", p.141), Courtney Han's road trip to her ancestral home ("Roots and Leaves", p.171) and tales from my own neighbors ("In the Hutong", p.196).

Perhaps the rhythm of the seasons best reflects the cyclical feeling of living in China. Foreigners come and go and come again, as do local friends swept along by the same currents. Some familiar news stories and features reappear in the papers every year. In Beijing, willow catkin pollen blows through the early spring air, and hillocks of cabbage appear in winter just ahead of the first frost. Only the smog endures.

After another few cycles, some of us won't be here anymore. We'll have moved back home or onto somewhere new, and all that remains of this moment in China will be the stories we tell of it. Others of us have made China our home, and aren't going anywhere (a sequel, *We're Still Here*, anyone?). We've long been disabused of the notion that we will ever "get" this country, let alone capture it in words. In the end it's too big a beast, and we're just flies resting on its back, witnessing what we can.

Alec Ash
Beijing, October 2015

MODEL WORKER

There's something about Fabien

Jonathan Rechtman

My CAREER AS a model started the way all good stories begin: I was walking down the street, minding my own business, when I was propositioned by a slim young Chinese woman with impeccable English, a snazzy white dress, and an attitude to match.

"You're perfect," she said, looking me up and down.

"Well, you've only just met me," I said. "But you're remarkably perceptive."

She ignored this, frowning. "Where are you from?"

"America," I said. "Where are you from?"

Again she ignored me. "I'd like you to call my boss. He is French. I think he would like to meet you. Here is his number," she said, handing me a soap-colored business card. "Please give him a call this afternoon. Tell him Angela gave you the card. Will you be in Chengdu for long?"

"About a month, maybe more."

She frowned again. She actually was quite ugly.

"Well, give him a call anyway. This afternoon. His name is Fabien."

And then she left, tossing her hair with a flick of her delicate, imperceptibly hairy wrist.

I bought a popsicle and sat on a bench to study the business card. The back had a snazzy logo with the letters "WMA" and a website address. The front read "Western Modeling Agency" and "Fabien Marc—Chief Agent/President/Model", with an office address and phone number. And there, in the lower-right corner, was a full-color head shot of Fabien.

The popsicle trembled in my hand. I sat, unmoving and unaware of time or space, paralyzed by the stunning good looks of the man that gazed back at me. Seductive, knowing, beckoning – cobalt eyes and stubble on a finely-sculpted chin, an irresistible come-hither aura projected at unseen women that would surely flock to his tanned, muscled body like iron filings drawn to a man-shaped magnet. This face could capture hearts with but a gaze, induce orgasms with but an expertly boyish wink. This was not a man, no, but a fanciful creation of the divine, a flesh-and-blood tribute to God and *GQ*.

I pulled out my cell phone and dialed the number on the card.

Two days later, on a hot afternoon downtown, I waited for Fabien at the south gate of Chengdu University. We had arranged to meet there and go back to his office nearby to "discuss the business" and "measure the model." In addition to being a heartthrob, I discovered on the phone that Fabien spoke an adorable brand of pidgin English.

I waited, perspiring heavily in the searing Sichuanese sun. Instead of my regular tank-top and shorts, I had dressed to impress with a pair of heavy black jeans and a button-down collared shirt. I was as uncomfortable as in-laws and sweating like guilt. I looked again at the business card, at Fabien's face, and felt a twinge of panicked excitement, like a high-school sophomore waiting for my prom date. He arrived on a motorcycle.

Blue chopper, white pants, navy shirt, purple shades. Silver chain. Hair gel and cologne. I discovered what the linguists already knew: the word "suave" is derived from French.

"Hello," he said. He looked me up and down as if I were a child, a mouse, an insignificant bug. "You are probably the Jon."

I tried to act cool and American. "Yeah," I said, pausing to take a James Dean drag on an imaginary cigarette. "You're Fabien, huh?"

"I am the Fabien. Hello. We will go to my office. Get on the back of the bike, yeah?" Was he mocking my "yeah"?

Five minutes later we pulled into a nearby apartment complex and climbed three flights of stairs, arriving at a door with a plaque: Western Modeling Agency. Fabien pulled out a ring with two keys, tried one, cursed, then tried the second, opening the door. "I live my house in the apartment next after the office," he muttered, cocking his pretty head down the hall. "Often the keys I choose wrong."

We entered the office, and I blinked hard. It was like someone had tried to imitate an expensive art gallery in Miami Beach using nothing but catalogue sales from Ikea — lots of white space with bright-colored, angular furniture and lamps that curved like snakes. From an adjacent room, European hip-hop played softly on computer speakers. The air-conditioner hummed like Zen. I discovered what the art historians already knew: "Art Deco" is derived from French.

Fabien led me into the other room, which consisted of a desk cluttered with papers and photographs, an assortment of bright pastel chairs and a comfy-looking sofa in zebra print. On the wall was a poster of Fabien posing shirtless with a Chinese girl in his arms. I chose a pink-lemonade colored chair and sat down.

"So first I will tell you about the Western Modeling Agency," he began. "If you want to be the model, you must know my company. Yes," he said, choosing his words carefully, "it is the most foremost modeling agency in the Chengdu city, probably in the Sichuan. If you want to be the model, you must know the

Western Modeling Agency, because my company is the only one that is good for Westerners."

Before I could respond, he veered into the hypothetical. "Maybe you are on the street, yes, maybe you are on the street today, and a man, a Chinese man, says to you: 'Oh you for my commercial please be the model! I will give you the money, here is the 100 *kuai*!' Maybe that will happen, yes? But I say no! I say you are the Westerner – the Westerner!" He beamed at me like he was saying the name of his child. "I say you are not worth the 100 *kuai*, you are worth the 1,000 *kuai*! You are worth the 3,000 *kuai*!"

I nodded sagely, letting the wisdom of his words sink in.

"Now," he said, narrowing his eyes and flashing me a winning smile. "It is time for you to answer the questions."

My anxiety and intimidation had vanished by this point, replaced by a playful amusement. Fabien, pretty as he was, seemed silly now—a nice-smelling man with a fondness for definite articles.

"First question. Why do you want to be the model?"

It was a tough one. I didn't know why I wanted to be the model, and I didn't know what motivations the model was expected to have.

"Vanity," I answered. "Ego tainted with a subtle insecurity."

"Vanity," Fabien repeated, looking worried. He had no idea what the word meant. He paused, looking down at a piece of paper in front of him, perhaps hoping it would offer a definition. Finally, he looked back up at me brightly.

"Second question: Are you confidence?"

"Oh I'm confident, baby," I said, figuring he'd like that. But Fabien only smirked. Your confidence is shit, that smirk said. It is *merde* compared to my confidence. I loved this guy.

"That's good," he said. "The model must be very confidence. But he must also be" – he paused for emphasis – "he must also be the photogenic!"

I nodded again, and he was pleased that I knew this word. "So," he said to me, "How do you look in the camera?"

As a matter of honest fact, I look terrible in almost every photograph that's ever been taken of me. Regardless of the location, lighting or lens, I invariably appear stoned, angry, salacious, sickly or dead. I most definitely am not the photogenic.

"I'm the photogenic!" I said. "I look great in pictures! Especially in China for some reason. It must be all the tea I drink here – it's really good for the skin, you know."

Fabien seemed satisfied. He got up from the desk and took a little roll of measuring tape from a drawer. It was time to measure the model. He measured my waist and shoulders, and entered the information on a sheet of paper. He asked me for my height and weight.

"Five feet, eleven inches," I said. "About a hundred fifty pounds."

He stared at me blankly. Fabien wanted meters and kilos. He also wanted the European equivalent of my shoe size. I had no idea how to calculate any of these numbers, and we finally had to resort to standing side by side, foot by foot, estimating the relative differences. The entire process was very demeaning.

"Okay," he said when he'd filled out all the spaces on his sheet. "You are good."

That was a relief. Measuring the model had been a lot harder than discussing the business, and I was glad it was over. "I think you will be the okay model, probably," Fabien concluded. "Now you must sign the contract."

He produced two stapled sheets of paper with WMA masthead and the company slogan: "WMA give you the opportunity style to make the fashion difference."

The contract was fairly simple. I, THE MODEL, agreed to

work exclusively for THE AGENCY in return for which THE AGENCY would create a photo-portfolio of me to show to THE CLIENT. When THE CLIENT selects THE MODEL to feature in an advertisement or fashion show (THE MISSION), THE AGENCY would negotiate the price and take thirty percent as commission.

I signed it immediately. Fabien signed too, and we shook hands, promising to be in touch in the next week to arrange a photo shoot. Then Fabien showed me to the door.

"Goodbye, Jon," he said. "Have the really nice day, okay?"

"You too, Fabien," I said. "I'll see you the later."

I never saw him again.

Many years have passed, but I still think of Fabien, and always with a smile. I still have my copy of the contract and business card, which I used to carry in my wallet so that his handsome face would never be far from my ass. If I'm ever feeling sad, I think of him lying on a fuzzy rug, straddling a motorcycle, or simply standing there, shirt open, a smirk on his lips and seduction in his eyes, his stubble fine and grey and deliberate, like pencil rubbed carefully on an artist's paper pad.

THE TIGER SUIT

Fiction

____

Tom Pellman

THE TIGER SUIT stinks. It smells like dried sweat and grass clippings. They make me wear it when we practice catching escaped animals at the Shijiazhuang Zoo. The last time, two weeks ago, they chased me for almost twenty minutes straight, waving their snares, until I fell into some bushes. I tore a small hole in the leg and now I have to remember to stay on Director Wang's right side so he doesn't see it. He says rules are rules. If the suit gets ruined when I'm wearing it, I have to pay for it. That's a rule. Another one is: last person who joined the team wears the suit.

"It's not fair," I whisper to Lao Li, who is sitting next to me in the back of the van. Lao Li is like my grandfather, but kind. "Why do I have to wear it? This isn't some training. This is the real thing."

Lao Li shrugs. "Ostriches are afraid of tigers."

I look down and stick a finger in the hole in my suit. "No, ostriches are afraid of people, with guns."

"Most people with guns," says Yu Zhong, loud enough for the whole van to hear. Everyone bursts out laughing.

"C'mon Hui Ming, of course you have to wear the suit," he goes on, tears still in his eyes. "If that bird ever sees your face again..." He can't finish, he's laughing too hard.

I try to ignore them by turning back to Lao Li and asking him about the bird. I've only seen it once and, yes, I was a little scared.

He says he doesn't know why the bird comes back to the same place every time it escapes. All he knows is that ostriches come from Africa, so it probably likes the sandy gravel out in the Hi-tech Zone, where everything is still under construction.

"But why does it always go there?" I ask, meaning the Oriental Pearl Hotel.

"It's a five-star hotel. He's got good taste."

Lao Li is pleased with this crack but everyone's done laughing. For the rest of the ride, I study Yu Zhong, watching how he leans back and stares out the window, cradling one of the guns in his arms like a child. He joined the zoo only two months before I did. He's never had to wear the suit.

When we pull up next to the Oriental Pearl Hotel, Director Wang yells for us all to wake up even though no one's sleeping. The scene outside looks like a storm blew through — tables overturned, bits of flowers trampled, a dirty red carpet. From inside the hotel, on the other side of the glass door, there's a row of people peering at us. Director Wang climbs out of the front seat and holds up both hands in greeting. *Meishi'r*, he yells.

Lao Li starts dividing up the gear — a black fishing net, three lengths of rope, a few long bamboo poles, a motorcycle helmet and the second gun. Yu Zhong slings his over his shoulder without discussion. Then he tucks his shirt into his camouflage pants. Everyone is wearing camouflage except for me.

"Where's your head, Hui Ming?" Director Wang says.

"Do I have to wear it? I can't really see."

"It's for your own protection."

"You won't scare the bird if you don't wear the head," Lao Li points out.

"At least give me a stick," I say, fixing the giant tiger head to my suit.

"We only brought three."

I turn away from them toward the building. Inside, a little boy is waving at me frantically. His face is beaming. I don't wave back.

"Can we just get this over with?" I say finally.

"What?"

No one understands anything I say when I wear the suit.

Director Wang turns from us and marches up the red carpet to meet the hotel manager scowling at the entrance.

"Just make sure he doesn't shoot himself this time," he calls over his shoulder.

Our little militia crosses the wide, empty road to the adjoining construction lot, the one where we found the bird last time. I walk behind them, one hand tugging down on my neck to keep the eye holes in place, the other gripping my tail like a hose. I've worn the suit enough times to know you have to keep it away from your feet.

"There!" someone shouts. A black blur shoots past on my left, close enough that I can hear its claws in the gravel. But by the time I swivel my head, it's gone. I can only make out silhouettes of earth-movers and cranes as we take crunching steps forward.

"He's back there," Lao Li whispers. "We need to flush him out into the open. Hui Ming? Where are you?"

"Here."

"The silent predator," Yu Zhong snorts.

I already know what Lao Li is going to ask me to do.

"And just remember," he finishes. "The bird is the one that's afraid of you. Just be careful of the claws. They're like a chicken's, but sharper."

The bird must have heard me coming because when I peek around the cement mixer, he's already standing at attention, head bowed, huge wings spread. When he starts hissing, I turn and give Lao Li a panicked look, which of course he can't see. Instead, I see Yu Zhong pointing his gun at his foot and pretend to shoot. My face turns hot with anger. They can't see that either, of course.

When the bird raises its head, it seems different. It looks ridiculous standing a full two meters tall on those plucked legs. Tiny head. Wild hair. Long eyelashes. What a stupid-looking animal! It has no idea what its put me through every day for the last six months. I can't say exactly why but I feel an urge to grab it by its delicate neck and squeeze. Yu Zhong doesn't believe I could do it. No one does. But I know I could kill it if I wanted to.

And then I'm charging toward the bird — screaming, groping, stumbling forward. I see a flash of fear in its giant eyes – I'm sure I see it – but it trots away easily when I'm still ten meters away. Once it's gone, I sit down on the dirt, take off my head and wipe away the sweat with my dirty paw.

The chase takes about twenty minutes but Yu Zhong is the one who finally shoots it, of course. By the time I join the others, they are standing in a circle around the thrashing bird, smoking, waiting for the dart's drugs to take hold. A few of them are still breathing heavy.

"That was harder than last time," someone says.

"Dumb fucking bird," Yu Zhong mutters. "Why does it keep doing this?"

Lao Li is squatting closest to it, inspecting its scratched neck. "He's not dumb. He's clever to have escaped so many times."

"It's dumb. So dumb it can't remember that it's got nowhere to go."

When we finally get it loaded into the van, Lao Li uses one of the ropes to lash a few sheets of newsprint around the bird's neck, to stop the bleeding. Its white tail feathers are stained red and brown. We tie the bird's legs together and someone puts a paper bag over its head.

"God, it looks like you've kidnapped it," Director Wang says when he sees us.

"It keeps him calm," Lao Li says. "He'll be fine."

For a few moments, we all listen to the bird's steady breathing, crinkling the paper.

Then, Director Wang yells.

"Hui Ming? Come out here!"

I feel my face get hot again, sure that he has finally seen the hole in my suit. I notice a group of children has followed Director Wang out of the hotel into the sunshine. They look cautious, half-frightened.

"No, Hui Ming, keep the suit on. Listen, I want you to stay here this afternoon. The kids love tigers. Stay and play with them for awhile. I owe the manager a favor."

I feel the crowd of squealing kids press in on me. One of them tugs at my tail. Director Wang is still talking to me, but I've stopped paying attention. For some reason, all I see is their delicate necks.

"Hui Ming? Are you listening? Where is your head?"

FLOWER TOWN

Rise and fall of a Sichuan village

Sascha Matuszak

I REMEMBER WHEN I learned my home was getting torn down. It was June 11, 2008, an exceptionally hot summer day. Flies were buzzing lazily around my head, and the shadows were sharper than knives. The women of the village, normally a chattering bunch, were conspicuously silent around the corner from my country house, hidden from view by the plum trees. I shuffled over to see what was going on, when a flimsy blue Chery QQ car flew around the corner.

The Chery jerked to a stop an inch from my bamboo clothesline. A man stepped out into the sunshine and looked around. Secretary Luo, one of the ladies breathed. In China, secretaries are the bosses and a boss in rural China is hard to mistake. Secretary Luo was portly, with shiny black shoes and a striped Burberry polo shirt. He had a thick head of black hair, a small smile on thick lips and cigarette stained skin. He had beady eyes that flicked back and forth across the scene. A driver, tall, lanky and balding, trailed his boss while nodding to himself and clutching a black leather bag in both hands.

I followed them to where the women were gathered in a small group, nervously waiting. These were strong women who worked alongside the men in the rose fields and gardens, tilling earth and sweating under the Sichuan sun. Women with powerful legs and gruff loud voices, who routinely invaded my courtyard, kitchen, home and bathroom to berate me for whatever it was I was doing. Now cowering with strained smiles and fearful eyes, they rocked their babies and nodded as Secretary Luo spoke.

"We're going to turn this place around, make it modern, you understand?"

The women nodded in unison. He swiveled on his heels and took in the small village.

"This is a great chance for all of you, you hear? There will be a meeting next week, we'll talk all about it there. This is a big deal for our village. We'll tear it all down in August."

He said it in the same tone as if he had mentioned the unusually clear skies on such a hot day. The lanky driver stood to one side and shuffled some papers, then looked up at no one in particular and licked his lips. With one more encompassing glance at the village and the women, Secretary Luo turned and strolled to his car.

"Alright then. Let's go."

With that they slipped back into their little blue Chery and sped off down the one-lane road that led through the village, forcing a vendor and his cabbage-laden motorcycle off to one side. The vendor narrowly missed the vegetables planted alongside the road and drove on, calling for us to "buuy cabbaage" in a nasal tone that carried across the sunbaked fields. I could still hear him as I turned to my neighbors, but they were pre-occupied. Their homes were being ripped out from under them in less than three months, along with the house I lived in, and I could see the shock spread across their faces in the noonday heat.

Chengdu, capital of Sichuan province, is the self-proclaimed birthplace of the *nongjiale*. The term translates literally as "farmhouse happiness" but has now come to mean both

Chinese-style bed and breakfast inns, and more figuratively the idyllic country life wealthy urbanites yearn for. The recent rise of farmer-run *nongjiale* alongside massive state-sponsored flower markets is nationwide, but it can be traced back to a genesis here, when farmers realized that by planting flowers and catering to city dwellers they could make ten times what they could growing traditional crops.

That's how places like *Sansheng Huaxiang* ("Three Gods Flower Village") came to be. A collection of small villages on the southeastern outskirts of Chengdu, in 2006 the municipal government designated *Sansheng Huaxiang* as an official flower-growing hub. The farmers had already changed much of their crop rotation to reflect the market – cabbage plots and cornfields became rose fields and pear orchards – and those with the means to do so turned their homes into B&Bs for the avant-garde Chinese middle classes who had begun arriving in droves since the mid 2000s. We called it Flower Town.

When I moved to Flower Town in September 2007, I rented a farmhouse in Unit 4 of 10,000 Fortunes village. The village ringed a large pond that attracted couples and photographers in the summer and lotus root hunters in the winter. The houses overlooking the pond all had a fresh coat of paint. The further you moved away from the water, the more mundane the homes were, until eventually they reverted back to standard country fare – raw concrete walls, a patchwork aluminum roof held down by bricks, and vegetable plots manning the perimeter.

Unit 4, a collection of 12 homes with about 50 people in total, sat on a small rise set back from the pond, surrounded by rose fields on all sides. Short, bow-backed men and women wandered from one plot to another, adding water from buckets suspended on a bamboo pole, pulling out weeds. Everyone was related, by blood or by marriage. About half of the village worked exclusively in the fields. The other half rented their plots out and worked in factories in the city. No one in Unit 4 operated a B&B except the village head.

On the far side of the rise was the hamlet's own smaller lotus pond, choked with mud and home to a family of geese. I could watch the geese from my upstairs window. Behind my house was a bamboo grove, with massive hornet-colored spiders hanging in the upper reaches. Bats whirled above the grove at night. It was a quiet place, and one of the few spaces in the village not covered with litter. A narrow concrete path led through fallow fields, around the rise, and over a tiny creek to the bus stop that connected Unit 4 with the wider world. On a clear day, I could see advancing columns of apartment complexes and office buildings. Most of them were empty shells, waiting for the urban wave to come crashing in and fill them up.

Farmhouses in China are not much better than empty shells themselves, and those in Unit 4 were no exception. Most were built of concrete and plaster, with minimal furniture, no insulation and not a single straight line in the whole building. The windowpanes were thin and rattled in their ill-fitting frames. There was no heating, and a typical country family keeps warm in winter by bundling up inside, watching television and sipping hot water.

Wang Meijie, my next door neighbor, was as an office worker in the nearby Pride cigarette plant. Her husband worked in a factory that built parts for motorcycles. Their 12-year-old daughter, Tiantian, was the first ambassador of the village to greet me when I arrived that September, ten months before Secretary Luo's fateful visit. She stepped across her mother's green rows of garlic and spring onions and demanded to know what in the hell I was doing in her village, so far away from all the other foreigners in Chengdu.

I told Tiantian that I wanted to get away from the city and work on a book. She sniffed at this, then went to inspect my furniture. I had little to speak of. I was so broke at the time that after paying three months rent for the place ($400) I had nothing left for furniture or appliances. Or food, for that matter. I had one rickety table, an electric heater and a few plates that I had cobbled together from friends. I also had a bag of rice and a bottle of soy sauce. She came out of my house looking as if she had seen a midget circus.

"You are out of your mind," she told me flat out, and hopped back over the garlic to go tell her mother about the dumb *laowai* next door who planned on sleeping on the floor and eating raw rice covered in soy sauce.

Later that night, Wang Meijie sent Tiantian to invite me over for dinner. We had braised fish, sliced potatoes with red peppers and some roast duck with rice. We ate pretty much in silence. They asked how much I was paying for my place. When I told them 10,000 yuan ($1200) for a year, they looked down at their bowls in an even more awkward silence than had pervaded the dinner up till then. After dinner, Wang's husband Li Guangwen handed me a smoke, and we went outside to sit. We smoked wordlessly as the sun set. The mosquitos rose up into the air, food for the bamboo grove bats, and the villagers retired to the corner store to gossip and play cards. For the first time in years, I saw stars above Chengdu.

The winter of 2007-08 was very harsh in Flower Town. The snowstorm that ravaged southern China left trains stranded during the Spring Festival, but closer to home, it almost froze Boogie Brown and me to death. Boogie was a musician with little money and a project to finish, so it seemed natural for him to join me in the countryside for solitude and inspiration.

We spent a lot of time huddled by the electric heater, wrapped in Tibetan cloaks we had bought in Western Sichuan years before, measuring the distance between our lips and the point where our breath disappeared. We lived off instant coffee, ramen noodles and the occasional meal scrounged up from scraps. There was nothing noble, adventurous or romantic about it. Being broke in China is pretty much rock bottom, and we knew it.

Every time the Nescafé ran out, I grew a little more depressed and less willing to return home to the country after a day of fruitless hustling in Chengdu. I ended up selling chunks of hashish to pay for bus rides and food. Every now and then Boogie taught an English class for a couple hundred yuan. I also taught English to a few students, sporadically. When they asked for their money back after several botched classes, I refused.

Salvation arrived in the form of a friend from the US who came to visit me in the middle of February. When he turned up, I held out my hands like an addict, oblivious to my own shame and his shock at having to bail me out. I piggy-backed off the money he had made fishing in Alaska the summer before, trading my knowledge of Chinese for his cash-flow. I took a trip with him to sunny Yunnan, and together we escaped my cold country home for a month. Boogie met a girl in Chengdu and moved in with her for a while, leaving our rental empty for the frigid months of February and March.

Spring was in bloom when I came back. Boogie was still in the city, making music. So I was alone when I found the doors of our empty house open and swinging in the wind. I walked inside to find dirt and garbage in the foyer, and spray paint scrawled up the staircase wall and into the second floor living area. My bedroom had the character for "fortune" sprayed onto the wall and Boogie's had "love" sprayed onto his. Somebody had pealed a peach and placed the peelings in a chalice inside the bottom drawer of a closet. I didn't find those peach peels until months later, after they had turned brown and slimy.

The vandalism didn't sting as much as the realization that I had become the "crazy cat lady" of the neighborhood, the target of all the little boys and girls. I was furious and hurt that my neighbors would do this to my home – who else could it have been? – and for days afterwards I wouldn't speak to anyone. The next month was quiet and tense. I didn't trust my neighbors, and they didn't know what to think of the *laowai* who came home at all hours of the night and sometimes not at all.

By then, Lhasa was burning and Kham, a Tibetan area of western Sichuan, was on lockdown. Riots in Tibet had led to a dozen police vans guarding the crossroads of the Tibetan district in Chengdu. The government-controlled media was letting everyone know that "foreign splittist elements" were trying to pry the Great Chinese Family apart. It was a bad time to be a foreigner in China, and even more so for me in the middle of a country village with no friends, no money and no idea what the people of Unit 4 gossiped about at the corner store. Although no one said a word to me, I imagined their looks and whispers whenever I went out to buy something, or passed them on the way to the bus stop.

There were, perhaps, other reasons for the tense atmosphere not apparent at the time. Scientists posit that subliminal foreshocks deep under the crust can cause birds and animals – and some humans – to act out, or flee. Did the dogs of the village bark more than usual during April 2008? Were the circling bats more frantic as the plates of the earth beneath them rubbed together and prepared to burst?

On May 9th, three days before the earthquake, I wrote this on my blog:

"A great many strange things have happened in the past

few days ... Perhaps not as many as may be transmitted by the feeling that accompanies one or two strange happenings, but nonetheless ... something is happening."

The next day, when the imperceptible foreshocks might have reached their climax, the gang of vandals that had assaulted my home while I was away stole a can of Krylon from my foyer and sprayed "Ma Shan is a Dork!" in huge blue letters right across the side of my house, using my Chinese name. I had taken a short walk to the store to grab a pack of Honghe cigarettes and some water, and when I returned the paint was still dripping.

It was broad daylight, and Wang Meijie was in her courtyard hanging up clothes. She had heard the rattle and hiss of the can. She knew who the punks were who had painted up my house. Watching her shake out sheets as if I wasn't there made me lose my mind. I whirled on her and Tiantian, and let loose with all of the invective I could muster.

I took a bottle of black ink and broke it on their house. I yelled at them and told them they knew who was doing this to me, but they wouldn't tell. Tiantian cried. Her mother defended her, searing my mouth shut with a look that reminded me of my own mother. I shrunk away back to my home, abashed at what I had said to a 12 year-old girl and her silent, shy mother. Minutes later I came out with a bucket of whitewash, and for two days I lathered paint over the offending black blotches. I never did get all of the black off their house. What happened next, on May 12, 2008, was China's most unifying catastrophe since the Japanese invasion. After the Wenchuan Earthquake struck, I walked dazed through the streets of Chengdu. Strangers chatted with each other. The parks and parking lots were full of families and groups of friends, listening to the radio, nervously chomping sunflower seeds. Never in all of my years in Sichuan did I feel more at home than during those minutes, hours and weeks after the quake tore a hole in the province and buried 80,000 people under rubble and metal and dust. I took several trips into the disaster area, and carried water up the hills. I wrote stories and took pictures. I sobbed in my room, thinking of children crushed and wailing.

My house out in Unit 4 became a fortress for many of my friends in the city. The village was 20km southeast of the city and the epicenter of the quake was 150km to the northwest, so everyone figured that in the weeks ahead, my place was the best spot to weather the daily aftershocks that rattled our ligaments and our neurons, making us all jumpy.

All was forgiven between me and my neighbors now – even if Tiantian still gave me the stink-eye – and they could not contain their curiosity. Now, instead of one lone *laowai* with a temper, there were ten to twelve of us at a time. Barbecuing. Playing music. Joking and running around with the village kids. The women spilled cautiously out of their homes and came to inspect our barbecuing technique, then politely, silently, took over for us. The whole village hung out late into the night.

We traded "where were you" stories with the gnarled rose farmers and ironmongers of the village, and chain-smoked until our throats went dry. The kids who were most likely responsible for my house resembling a hobo lair went back and forth to the corner store for beer and smokes. They sat around us and listened, sharing our food.

Just a couple weeks later, Secretary Luo's blue Chery QQ came sputtering to halt in my courtyard and everything changed.

When Zhou Sushen was little, all the pretty girls bound their feet. As an adult, while she bent over day after day and pulled weeds and food from the soil, China went through the political convulsions of a lunatic. Every so often she would stand up and steady her back with one hand, ankles deep in mud, and listen as the local Party Secretary rolled through Unit 4 and blared details of the most recent campaign through a bullhorn. As the years went by, the messages of the cadres became increasingly arcane and indecipherable. Confused and trusting, she learned to just nod her head approvingly.

"Our Secretary Luo would never lie to us," she declared to the group of worried women that had gathered in the wake of the announcement. "The government will take care of us."

Nobody looked convinced. Countless horror stories involving greedy developers, duplicitous politicians and desperate peasants had made the villagers nervous. Would they be compensated fairly? Would there be apartments waiting for them here when it was all finished? Would the government help them find new homes in the interim?

Secretary Luo had promised the villagers that they would only have to move elsewhere for two years, and then they would be moved back to Unit 4, to live in apartments – 30 square meters per person. In the interim, the government would pay 600 yuan per month to each family as well as a lump sum based on the value of the house.

Zhou's nephew, Li Fafu, was doubtful.

"It's hard to say what they will do with this land," he said. "This is good land and it's in a prime location. I can't imagine that they would let us back on here after they get us off. Especially if they can make millions doing something else. The government doesn't want farmers anymore. We'll see what they say at the meeting."

The meeting took place at the house of the village head, Deng Weixin, on June 15 2008, at 10am. Everyone seemed excited that morning, almost playful. I had butterflies in my stomach. I was expecting a showdown between the peasants and the politician-developer bad guys over the future of Unit 4. I might even keep my home, I thought to myself, as I skipped across the rose fields to Deng's sprawling white concrete house, which doubled as one of the best B&Bs in the area.

Secretary Luo, his lackey Mr Zhou and six other officials sat outside the house, at a long table under a grove of plum trees. The villagers gathered in a semi-circle facing the table. Children scampered around and picked plums off the ground, wiping them clean and taking big, juicy bites. The men ringed the back of the gathering, smoking and chatting, occasionally shaking a small tree and enjoying the plums that fell. After a few minutes, Mr Zhou stood up and gave the opening speech.

"The municipal government has decided to modernize the facilities of all villages in accordance with the central government's plans to develop the countryside and enrich the farmers. The re-development and construction phase will begin in August and will last two years. In these two years, all residents of 10,000 Fortunes, Unit 4 will be compensated with a monthly stipend. Furthermore, the municipal government has ordered the developers to build a new, modern apartment complex to house all of the villagers of 10,000 Fortunes, Unit 4. Each resident will be given 30 square meters per head, which for most families equals 90 square meters, to compensate for the loss of their homes and fields. This can be allocated according to your wishes. Furthermore, the government will pay each resident a lump sum based on the amount of land owned, the extent of development of each parcel, the type of cultivation currently on each parcel, and also the size of each dwelling."

Murmurs rolled through the crowd and a few of the women yelled out, demanding to know the details of the payment process. Mr Li, Vice Secretary of the district, the next level of government up, stood to address the crowd. He was a young man with an intelligent expression and close-cropped hair. Of all the officials present, he was also the only one not chain-smoking.

"Good afternoon comrades, I am glad all of you are here for this important meeting and I am happy to be here as well. This is a very important day for Flower Town, as well as 10,000 Fortunes, Unit 4. The government is modernizing and developing this area and soon this will be a bustling center of commerce with schools and playgrounds for your children and business opportunities for your families. The city of Chengdu is developing very quickly and soon not only will the Third Ring Road be developed, but the Fourth Ring will surely be modernized as well in the coming years. Our China is growing rich and the government is bringing these riches to the countryside as is dictated in the five-year plan recently agreed upon in Beijing. All of you will receive fair compensation for your homes and land and you will be able to live here forever in nice, modern homes provided to you by the government in return for your sacrifice. This area will become even more beautiful as modern development techniques are utilized to keep the water clean, protect the fields and provide electricity and even the Internet for the entire area."

At the end of his speech, Mr Li gave the villagers a chance to ask questions and speak their piece. No one moved at first, then one lady rose up and started talking. Her voice shook and her face reddened as she gained momentum.

"I have lived here all my life. My mother and father are old and sick and live with me too. My husband is a laborer in the city and I work in the fields. We have no money. How are you going to compensate me for losing my home? What am I supposed to do for two years while I wait for you to finish this building? How do I even know that I will have a place here in two years? I know you will change things midway. How are we supposed to live in the city with those high rents and no skills? I'm a farmer. I want to know right now how much money I can get for my fields and how much money you are going to pay me each month and how are you going to guarantee that I receive my money each month. I can't sign away my life to you. We know you officials and developers don't care about us."

Other villagers chimed in with similar stories and began crowding the table. Mr Li nodded and asked everyone to calm down. But the villagers were getting restless, and repeatedly called for details about the one-off sum each family will receive, the amount of monthly compensation and how long it would take to get paid. Then one of my neighbors, Guo Xiulan, pointed at me and yelled out, "Let the *laowai* speak!"

I had told my neighbors before that I would speak on their behalf. All of the villagers stepped away from me and started clapping, then went silent as I cleared my throat and began.

"Hi, my name is Ma Shan. Most of you know me already, but for those who don't, I am the only *laowai* who lives out here and I have been here for about ten months. I moved out here because this area is beautiful and peaceful. I love living here. I have come to know my neighbors and you have all taken me in as one of your own and treated me very well. When we heard that the village was going to be torn down it was a great shock and also a big disappointment. All over China places like this are being torn down to create apartment blocks and to make way for the city. There is no place for anyone to go and see the beauty of this country anymore because the cities just keep growing. Is it really necessary to tear this place down and make another city? There is great potential for tourism here if we can just maintain what we have and keep it pristine and natural. If you develop this place, you might regret it in a few years when this becomes just another dirty, crowded city suburb. My neighbors love this place and this is their home. I urge the government to consider maintaining 10,000 Fortunes as it is and focusing on tourism and bed and breakfast revenue. I hope you can keep the environment here as it is."

I faltered and went silent. I realized halfway through that my arguments were senseless and falling on deaf ears. Not even the peasants entertained any thoughts of "keeping things natural" or any hope of making money with a bed and breakfast business. Progress was a foregone conclusion and the real crux of the argument was not whether or not to proceed, but how much money was going to be paid out and when the payments would happen. The villagers clapped and cheered, but I knew in my heart that I was a clown.

Mr Li got up to answer.

"We know that Westerners enjoy the rural beauty of China. That is why we are keeping all of this area exactly how it is. The government has promised that Flower Town and 10,000 Fortunes will always be available to our foreign friends. We are committed to a Green City and to green development. The apartment building will take up only a little bit of space and it is there to house the villagers. Their homes will be torn down to make way for a large park and beautiful villas that will be rented out and sold to foreign friends like this *laowai*. We welcome you to return to Flower Town in two years, Mr Ma Shan, and I am sure you will love what we have done with the place."

As soon as he finished, the arguing started back up over the terms of payment. At first, Mr Li waved them down and tried to continue, but the din grew so loud that the officials had to stand up and yell the crowd down. A phalanx of women crowded the table and slammed their hands down, shrieking at the officials to provide details. Eventually, Secretary Luo waded into the middle of the fracas and shouted his villagers into submission. He took over from Mr Li and delivered a succinct speech, waving a sheaf of papers as he shouted.

"No one here is going to walk away without their proper amount of cash, don't worry about a thing. But until every last one of you signs this document here, releasing your home to the developers and confirming that you accept the government's generous offer, no one is getting paid anything!"

"We've been through this before," mumbled one old peasant as he handed me a cigarette on the way back to Unit 4. "They talk big and promise everything, but a year from now the money will be gone. Then what are we supposed to do, huh?"

I shrugged, lit his smoke for him and walked back home through the rose fields.

I wish I could tell you that the village banded together in defiance against the bigwigs to demand justice and compensation, but that isn't what happened. We just lived out the last days. One by one, all of the families signed their homes away, took what cash they could and moved out.

Several families moved to Luojia Alley, the outskirts of a town that itself was the outskirts of a bigger town. The space between Unit 4 and Luojia Alley is just a jumble of overgrown fields, stacks of bricks and crumbling ruins. Other families went further afield. Wang Meijie, Li Guangwen and Tiantian left for Longcuan, a larger town farther south where Wang had a sister with extra rooms.

The weeks that followed the meeting filled me with resignation. In July, I got a job working for a security firm in Beijing during the Olympics. I had been trying to get hired for months, and I was happy and relieved to finally have some gainful employment. If I took the job, I would miss the bitter end of Unit 4, when the bulldozers would finally come and destroy the village where I lived. If I didn't take it, I would go hungry and miss the Olympics. I didn't hesitate.

In Beijing I scalped tickets, watched Serena Williams play tennis, and got paid. At the end of August I flew back to visit my old home, to see what had happened. I had moved most of my things into a new apartment in Chengdu before leaving for Beijing, so going back to the countryside was just indulging my curiosity.

I pulled into the courtyard of my farmhouse late at night. The headlights of the yellow cab illuminated a gutted building and piles of scrap wood. Unit 4 had become a dark world of shadows and scavengers. I saw two men with flashlights stumbling out of my front door. One had bits of rope and string in his hands. The other was carrying two baskets of broken metal and wood. I saw one of my flip-flops in his basket. Piled on their truck were the drawers of my old closet and a mattress I had left behind.

As I looked around at the destruction the night looters had wrought, my chest grew constricted and cold. The windows of my old home were Wang Meijie's gouged out eyes; the doors, tattered frames half stripped of nails swinging in the wind, were fading memories of children screeching as they played. Sunlight on a guitar string. Wisps of long black hair. Li Guangwen washing his motorbike with a toothbrush. A cigarette. Drinking with Li Fafu. His laugh. Roses. Lamplight on a gathering.

Today, Unit 4 is one large fallow field. The small pond where herons used to skewer frogs is filled with mud and dirt. A few puddles belch out mosquitos into the humid air. The rose fields that once surrounded us have given way to weeds and scrub. Yellow foam padding lies piled up where my house was, and a few bowls and bottles speak of the squatters who gather here at night, still scavenging the ruins perhaps, or just drinking under the moon.

Li Zhongwen, one of the elders of the village, tills the fields were his house once stood. He grows "bashful plants", so named because if you poke them, the leaves curl in on themselves. He sells the plants for eight *mao* a stem at the local flower market, and harvests onions and greens for his home.

"The government isn't doing anything with this land," he told me in July 2012. "So we'll keep tilling it until they make a move."

My old neighbor, Li Dongmei, sits in her living room two years after her home was torn down, and looks at old pictures with me. She tells me that the monthly stipend of 600 yuan ended two months ago. She was promised a lump sum of 15,000 yuan, but it was split into three payments. She has only received 5,000 yuan of it so far, enough to pay for a year's rent on her current place, above a small convenience store a few blocks down from Unit 4. I wonder out loud why a rich developer would split such a small sum into three installments. She raises her head and I see that the thought had never occurred to her.

"Nobody speaks for us, nobody cares about us," she says listlessly as her daughter does homework on the bed. "Here we are renting this tiny place ... it's sad. We used to have a home."

When we talk about Unit 4, she is forgetful, irritable, indifferent. She is more interested in my life. Where I work, how much money I make. We go through the rest of my old pictures from the village and then she waits, in silence, for me to finally take my leave.

WRITERS IN CHINA

Poetry

Anthony Tao

Fling a bottle any direction
and likely you'll hit a writer
who thanks you
for the drink.

Archivist of residuum
and flumadiddle,
quidnunc of
the inconsequential,

tapping into Evernote
words of cabbies
as in cantos,
The China Experience.

How we hope
our lives are more
than the hottest pub or club,
contours of new beds,

or whispers of sex
in a UNIQLO fitting room,

keeping silent when another asks,
Who hasn't?

Who amongst us
would not write our destruction
if it meant, between self-
published covers,

we could be cavalier
streaking down the day
with first-world swagger,
our sense of the just

hot in our judgmental hearts?
Look at those self-flagellating diarists
grinning uneasily into the crowd
at open mics:

Do they write for themselves or us?
Perhaps you know, sitting there.
How lonely the hours can be, even here,
when you're looking into no mirror.

Examining the Past

Personal history

Karoline Kan

FOR YEARS, I felt spite for my father. In my eyes, he was the most irresponsible dad in the world. He didn't earn enough money to support us. He didn't enjoy family gatherings, and was always the first to leave the table. He didn't care whether his kids were happy in school or not, but would be angry if we didn't perform as well as he expected. He often quarreled with my mother, for reasons I didn't understand.

"Who can you blame? It's your own fate!" my mother would shout at him. Father would stay silent, turn to the other side of the room and light a cigarette, while my mother again told me the story from more than thirty years ago, which in her mind had led to father's bitterness. Through the cigarette smoke, I remember seeing tears in his eyes as mother reminded him of the old pain.

My father was born in the summer of 1957, the first boy in a conservative family in a village near Tianjin. Life was hard, but he was loved and spoiled by the whole family. My grandfather had never been to school, which became his life's regret, so he projected all his old hopes onto his son. "Nothing in the world is as noble as being an intellectual," he would tell his neighbors. They didn't understand why he never made his son do farm work, and instead let him read novels, poems and comic books, or listen to an old radio broadcasting the latest international news, while his peers labored on the farmland for their families in that poverty-stricken time.

Father didn't let his family down. He had a good memory, and did well in school. My grandmother told me that one day in math class, the teacher couldn't solve a question, but my father raised his hand and gave the embarrassed teacher the answer, using a formula that hadn't been taught in class yet. In his countryside school, that story made my father a kind of legend. Since then he was given the nickname "Hua Loo Keng the Second", after the famous Chinese mathematician. They still call him that in his hometown.

There wasn't much entertainment in China's countryside in the 1960s and 70s. My father spent most of his time reading the classics: *Romance of the Three Kingdoms*, *The Art of War*, *The Water Margin*. He enjoyed telling the stories to a group of young boys who would follow him around, while my grandfather planted the rice, cut the weeds and fed the horse. People joked, "The old farmer has a city son." Hearing this, my grandfather would just smile and say proudly, "He is a good student.My father never regarded himself as a member of the village. People said he was arrogant. In his heart, he didn't see the other young villagers as his friends; he just liked being admired by them. He made jokes about them, and thought up nicknames which became popular, like "Duck Zhang" for the guy whose voice sounded like a duck, "Little Fifth Potato" for a fifth son who was short with dark skin, or "Mao the Second" for the kid who admired Chairman Mao so much that he kept the same hair style as the young Mao Zedong, and always had two Little Red Books in his pocket.

During the Cultural Revolution, the key years of my father's education, classes in school were suspended, or replaced with special cultural and labor education classes. Those children who didn't like to study found themselves in paradise, but others, like my father, never gave up studying and waited for their chance.

In 1966, when my father was still in primary school, the *gaokao* was stopped. Mao Zedong wrote in *People's Daily* in 1968: "Education should emphasize revolution [and] serve proletarian politics." In the 70s, university was only for farmers, workers and soldiers. Family background was an important factor, as well as your ability and "political consciousness". My father thought he had a chance, but he was wrong. The system was based on recommendation, and since none of his family members were cadres, Party members or Red Guards, my father wasn't nominated. In 1975, he finished high school. But he couldn't believe the door was totally closed.

On October 21, 1977, the *gaokao* was reinstated. This rekindled my father's dream of going to university. He prepared hard for the exam, which would take place one month later, and was confident he would be the first university student in the family. On that winter day, my grandfather took his son to the examination building in his horse carriage, and waited outside in the cold for hours. It was the only *gaokao* in Chinese history that took place in winter, and the one with lowest enrolment ratio. Less than 300,000 students were enrolled from more than 5.7 million students.

His result was good. My father was accepted by a prestigious medical university, to major in surgery science. But while he was preparing for the first semester, some family members changed their minds. A doctor? they thought. Doctors are just like servants, serving patients. Will he end up being a barefoot doctor, carrying his medicine box from village by village like a fraud cheating villagers into buying his medicine? The discussion confused my grandfather, who couldn't accept that his son would be just a "patient server" in the villagers' eyes. He told my father, "I don't allow you go to this university. Prepare for next year's *gaokao*, do it again, and let's have a better plan for your major."

In the summer of 1978, my father took the *gaokao* for the second time. This time, his score was even higher. He chose a science university, to major in physics. But a few days later, an official from the local education bureau told my father that there was a new policy, and those who were enrolled last year but didn't go were disqualified this year as punishment. "Our country has very limited education resources," he said. "So I can't send your materials to the university."

Nobody knows if what the official said was the truth. In that era everything was in a mess, and it's hard to say if there really was such a policy, or if there were other reasons behind it. Rumor had it that the official was newly appointed to his position and wanted to do something. Others said that the official's niece performed worse in the exam but applied to the same major in the same university, and it's not possible for two students from the same high school to both be accepted, so my father was sacrificed.

My father wanted to have a third try in 1979. This time, before he even registered for the *gaokao*, he was refused on account of being overage. He was 22. It was the death sentence for his future. When I think of what my father went through, my heart bleeds for him.

I have a box for the special things I value most. In it there are two things that belonged to my father. One is a black and white photo from his high school student card. He wasn't handsome, but he had the air of someone who is well educated, a bit shy, in a black uniform commonly seen in that time. The other is a draft of a play script he wrote in school. His handwritten characters in dark blue ink are elegant, and at the end it says, "By Tai, 1972".

I had collected both items from a pile of old books in my

grandfather's house in the early 2000s. I still remember how shocked I was when I found them. I couldn't believe they belonged to my father, the man who in my eyes was boring and weak, whose hobbies were smoking, playing poker and Chinese chess, and drinking beer. The man who, for as long as I could remember, seldom smiled, never hugged or kissed me, or talked to me about my joys and sorrows, hopes and fears. The only thing that ever cheered him up was when I got another first place result in the school exams.

I loved it when my father got drunk, because it was the only time when he became talkative. He liked to talk about politics and history, and one time he wrote a poem. I remember the last two lines: "I don't have the courage to look back twenty years / In my dreams the scent of books cuts me dead."

In 1979, when my father was excluded from university for the final time, he allowed himself to sink into the mire of his own self-pity. The other villagers thought he had gone mad. He became very silent, and for days he left home every morning, coming back when it got dark. Some of the villagers said sarcastically, "he believed he was a phoenix but turned out to be a chicken, no different from other country chickens."

One day in that late autumn, my grandmother told me, my father disappeared for two days. Some people in a neighboring village said they saw a silent young man sitting alone on the riverbank. My father's family went crazy looking for him, afraid that he would jump in, but he came back on the third day, with a pale face and purple lips. Nobody knows what happened, but after that my father seemed to accept his new fate. He locked all of his books in the warehouse, together with his once beautiful dreams.

Within a month, my grandfather sent him to the farm to learn everything from scratch. Over the years, my father did all kinds of work – farming, trading, running a kindergarten with my mum. But he never felt passionate about any of it. Most of the time, he depended on my mother to make all the big decisions. When I was five, we moved from the village to a bigger town nearby. "I missed the best age," he told me later, "the best opportunities, the best everything." Back then I thought it was just an excuse for his laziness. Now I understand it as a helpless self-consolation.

I have said a lot of things that hurt my father's feelings. I told him that he didn't love our family. But as I grow older, I have gradually come to forgive him. I am trying to understand my father. If I were him, could I have done it better? I don't know.

The day when I took my *gaokao* in the summer of 2008, it was raining. As I came out at the end, I saw my father waiting for me outside the school in the rain, one hand holding an umbrella and in the other a bag of my favorite cakes and fruit. I again thought of my father's story, and noticed for the first time that he was getting old. I turned my face away from him, and started silently to cry.

The View

Flash fiction

Josh Stenberg

Jason called out of the blue. He was staying at a fancy hotel in Pudong; I should come over. The view was amazing, he said. Had I ever been? So, come.

I was so startled that I almost stumbled in the street. I agreed instinctively, out of confusion. Once I put down the phone, a prick of self-loathing. I wasn't going anywhere special, so I bought a pair of new shoes in self-parody. Leather is also a kind of substance abuse.

Despite the shoes, the day was suddenly empty and smelled perilous. There was too much time before I was to go meet him and I knew that at home I would only mull and stew. So I just kept walking. The streets were cradled in that brief spring when the temperature is still comfortable but the threat of summer has already made the rounds. Things begin to sweat, especially things like us, who don't belong, who prickle and rash. The climate is trying to excrete us.

This thought proved I hadn't slept enough, so I repressed the desire for a cigarette and groped about in my mind for some duty or escape. I followed a sign, as if it held some kind of authority, like it might fulfill a perverse need to foil expectation. I turned into the Sun Yat-sen residence.

It was a shady courtyard, with the usual garrulous security

guards and a dejected woman in the ticket box. Everything had the appearance of normality even though Jason was in Shanghai and had summoned me. Inside there were so many pictures of Sun Yat-sen and Soong Meiling, and even one of George Bernard Shaw – all this even though Jason had called me and was in Shanghai. Evidently the world had existed for eternities, holding railway revolutions and studying medicine in Hawaii and failing to unify a country, all without reference to Jason and me.

I finally broke down in front of a bookcase in Sun Yat-sen's study. Each volume of the classical history was a different size, and they fit into the case like a puzzle. I tried to convey something of this mystery to an Australian girl in shorts who asked me if I was all right.

"To think of all the time great men spend doing stupid things," I said, sniffling.

I went into the gift shop and only then understood why I had come; why, it was now clear, I had been sent here. Jason would ask what I had done with my day, and the answer would be respectable, passable. Now I had gone to the Sun Yat-sen residence. I would say it and it would even be true. I marveled at my unconscious foresight. I even bought a book about the revolution, to remind Jason of his insufficiencies and vanities, his smallness.

When I came out it was raining, and I took off my new shoes. I went back home and put newspaper in the shoes and thought of how little I should be thinking about Jason, until it was time to go meet him, by which time he seemed very distant indeed.

He wasn't in the lobby. I phoned from downstairs, but he made me go right up to his room in the elevator, like a whore. I should have dressed more modestly. There was an elevator girl, a profession I didn't think existed anymore. Her badge said her name was Maroon. Standing at the back of the mirror, I watched her eyes in the dull reflection of the elevator metal for seventeen floors, judging her back in revenge for my assumption that she was judging me. I reached Jason's floor and his door and there was a hug, of course, and also a pat. Ambiguities exchanged.

Luxury is never as luxurious as you think. He's a big deal, it seems, but the room was puny. Shanghai is so dense that even rich people are squeezed; small are my revenges. I murmured something about it being less than spacious. He laughed. He poured us tea, tacky tea, from bags.

At least he showed me to the window, not to the bed. "It's the best view in Shanghai," he said, "You've never seen Shanghai like this." It was true enough; we were high up. Shanghai did its pulsing and weaving and clogging, like the heart of an extravagantly fat man.

"You can't even see the people from here. Just lights and darkness."

"But isn't it incredible?"

"I bought you a book." I said, clapping it on the teak. "A hundred years ago this was still the Qing Dynasty. Can you imagine? Shanghai was nothing, or close to nothing." I put my hand on his knee.

He said, "You're not even looking at the view. It's like it's not even there. Look at where we are."

"It's still the city. You're here." I swallowed, then dared, "You can't make love to a city."

"From what I hear, you've been trying."

Instead of throwing the tea in his face, I smiled, as if it was a funny joke. "Are we going somewhere from here?" I asked.

He looked at his cell phone and it turned out he had plans. He had forgotten. He had just wanted me to see the view; the best view in Shanghai. It had been good to see me. He would not have forgiven himself if he had let me miss the best view in Shanghai.

THE BOOK OF CHANGES

Jazz with Chinese characteristics

David Moser

"WHAT DO YOU miss most about the US?" asked my friend Chen Xin, pouring me another beer.

"Nothing," I said. It was 1993, and I was living in Beijing, yet even when drunk I was never homesick for America.

"There must be something," she said, licking the excess foam off my glass.

"Jazz."

The next day I called up her friend Liang Heping, a pianist. He told me that yes, there was a *jiemu saishen* ("jam session") that weekend, and I was welcome to sit in. I was a failed jazz musician who had studied music at Indiana University, struggled to survive playing gigs in Boston for years, then finally given up to go into a field I was sure would bring in the big bucks: Chinese linguistics. I had assumed I would never have a chance to play jazz again, yet here I was in 1990s Beijing, where every week something that couldn't possibly happen happened. A friend loaned me a battered Chinese trumpet, and I set out from Peking University, taking one of the infamous yellow death-trap "breadbox taxis" to Maxim's.

Maxim's was a French-style bistro plunked rather improbably into the middle of Beijing. (Or at least it was improbable in 1983 when Pierre Cardin, the French couturier, opened the bar declaring "If I can open a Maxim's in Beijing, I can open one on the moon!") When I showed up the place was almost empty, just a few French tourists clustered at a table, ignoring the jazz band completely. I sat at a table and listened as the musicians finished their first set with Charlie Parker's "Now's the Time", which seemed appropriate. As they took a break, I went up to Liang Heping.

"Welcome," he said, "We're absorbing a little of your country's spiritual pollution here." Liang was tall with hippie-length hair, while the drummer, Liu Xiaosong, had a punk-rock buzz cut hairstyle and an earring, something shockingly *outré* in China at that time. By contrast, the tenor saxophonist, Du Yinjiao, with his clean-cut looks and well-toned body, looked more like a PLA soldier. As it turns out, he was.

"I'm a soldier in the People's Liberation Army band in Beijing," he told me, "We're not supposed to take jobs outside of our army unit, but sometimes I sneak out of the base and play at these jam sessions."

I asked him what his normal duties were in the PLA band. "Well, this afternoon I played the national anthem at the Great Hall of the People for Jiang Zemin, and tonight I'm playing Charlie Parker here." Du told me he had learned jazz by listening to Voice of America shortwave broadcasts in the 80s.

"You've heard of Benny Goodman?" he asked me. "It's difficult to figure out his music by listening to the radio. That's why we like it when a foreigner comes along. Do you have any tapes of his music I can borrow?"

I took the stage for the next set, and they asked me what tunes I wanted to play. I noticed that on the music stands they all had tattered copies of *The Real Book*, the Bible of jazz musicians, a copyright-violating book with the melodies and chord changes for hundreds of standard jazz tunes. When jazz musicians improvise, they do so over the succession of chords that underlie the melody, and call it "playing the changes." Ironic, I thought to myself, that the culture that produced the ancient divination classic the *Book of Changes* had now imported this musical book of changes. I suggested we play Sonny Rollins' tune "Airegin", and he announced to the group "Okay, page 11!"

I had assumed I would have to learn a lot of jazz jargon in Chinese, but it turns out that for jazz, as for other Western imports in China, English is still the lingua franca. In the middle of fast-paced Chinese they sprinkled English phrases like "bossa-nova", "swing feel", "trade fours" and "bass line". I was a bit rusty on the borrowed trumpet, but it was fun to be in the groove again. The tempo was uneven, Liang Heping's accompaniment on the keyboard was more Rachmaninoff than Bill Evans, but still – it was *jazz*.

I suddenly had a sense that time and space had contracted, that Beijing had truly become part of the global village. After the set, the bass player told me how much he liked Miles Davis, calling him "Miles" in the same way that an American jazz aficionado would. I was jolted out of my *kumbaya* moment when he asked me, "Did Miles ever play Dixieland?" It was an odd question, since Dixieland predated Miles Davis by decades.

"Well, I don't think so," I said, "though he did have a great admiration for Louis Armstrong."

"Who?"

Another musician sat in during the next set, a diminutive fellow in a tie-dye t-shirt on the flugelhorn (a mellower cousin of the trumpet). He played with more expression and originality than the other musicians, though it was clear he had not studied jazz theory. I thought he looked familiar, but couldn't quite place him. My puzzlement was dispelled when the drummer pulled me over to the newcomer. "The two of you should meet," he said. "David, this is Cui Jian."

The next week I was in Cui Jian's apartment, giving him some jazz theory tips. A slight, soft-spoken young man, he would not have struck me as the iconoclastic godfather of Chinese rock. When I was at Peking University in the late 80s, his song "Nothing to My Name" played constantly on tinny dorm room cassette players, and later became the anthem of the 1989 Tiananmen Square student protest movement. I knew Cui Jian played the trumpet, but I had no idea he was a jazz enthusiast.

"Are you thinking of branching out into jazz?" I asked him.

"I can't really play it yet," he said, "but at least jazz is safe to perform here. It's hard for me to get approval for concerts in Beijing, and even outside of the city I get banned all the time."

The events of June 4th still resonated in the capital, and the politics of rock music were very much a topic of discussion. Chinese youth naturally felt a spiritual affinity with rock, and there were a few indigenous groups such as Tang Dynasty and Black Leopard that played for passionate fans across the country. Jazz was almost completely off the radar, but Cui Jian nevertheless saw potential for it.

"Rock is very direct, it's good for shaking people up," he said. "Jazz is subtler. It requires a longer time to take hold, but the effect on the spirit can be deeper. I believe it can also raise Chinese people's political consciousness." I reminded him that Miles Davis had once said, "Jazz is the big brother of revolution. Revolution follows it around." He laughed.

"Right. They say rock-and-roll is subversive, but from what I've read, jazz was really the music that brought down the Berlin Wall."

"And now, the Great Wall?"

Jazz had come to China. Or more accurately, it had returned. After all, Shanghai nightlife in the 1920s and 30s included jazz as a part of the cultural mix. Dozens of African-American jazz musicians traveled by steamboat to China to seek gigs in the freewheeling international club scene. Buck Clayton, who later on would play trumpet with Count Basie, formed his first jazz band in Shanghai. And local Chinese musicians absorbed it all to create a form of jazz with Chinese characteristics, a hybrid of New York's Tin Pan Alley and Shanghai pop songs.

When I first got to Beijing in 1986 there were still fossils of this pre-Liberation Chinese *faux* jazz, such as a group who called themselves *Lao Shupi*, "Old Tree Bark." The band members were all in their sixties and seventies (the drummer had a hearing aid, as I recall) and performed a style of jazz somewhere between corny and incoherent. American trombonist Matt Roberts had already made valiant pioneering efforts to assemble something like a genuine American jazz ensemble. And a German bassist, Martin Fleischer, had pulled together a group of Chinese and foreigners calling themselves the "Swinging Mandarins," who provided passable cocktail jazz in the main lobby of Beijing's Jianguo HotelBy the time I discovered Chinese jazz in the 90s, the influx was still a trickle, not a wave. As I became a part of the subculture, I found out that the musicians were still unfamiliar with jazz harmony, and needed chord-playing instruments – piano, guitar – more than trumpets and saxophones. I began to play piano at the gigs, even though I had never really studied piano. My technique was pathetic, but I was competent enough in jazz harmony to provide reasonable "comping" (the jazz term for accompaniment), and transcribe musical arrangements and charts.

The musicians were also woefully unfamiliar with the basic repertoire of tunes. I once played a hotel gig with a bass player who after the first set of jazz classics confessed, "You know, I've never heard any of the tunes we just played. Do you have any tapes of them?" Jazz tapes and CDs were very scarce in those pre-Internet days, and players hoarded them like sacred relics. In fact, one of the most common complaints I heard was that musicians refused to share their precious stash with anyone else, for fear that others would benefit from the musical "secrets" therein and get an edge on them.

And yet, they were all drawn inexorably to the music. Jazz has always tended to be "music for musicians," and this was no exception in Beijing. Players congregated at clubs with little or no audience and zero pay, just to be part of the buzz. Bass player Huang Yong, a staple of weekend jazz sessions, told me, "When I discovered jazz, it changed my entire view of music. Pop music has limits, but jazz is about reaching an unattainable goal. But that's what's so frustrating. Why is it that our improvised solos never sound as good as the recordings? What are we missing?"

This was a question that came up time and again: When would China produce a soloist with a distinctive voice, an individual style? I discussed this with Liu Yuan, Cui Jian's saxophone player, during breaks at the CD Café, Beijing's first jazz club. Liu had begun as a child learning the *suona*, a double-reed Chinese folk instrument, and had switched to sax after hearing a jazz group in Hungary. When he returned to China, he taught himself jazz by listening on repeat to the only jazz tape he owned, a Grover Washington, Jr. album.

"Chinese jazz has yet to find a solo voice," Liu lamented. "Jazz should be pure expression, but we're too hesitant to express ourselves. I think it goes to a basic cultural difference. We just don't have a tradition of individualism. I feel this flaw in my own playing, too. I always hold back, afraid of playing wrong notes."

I told Liu the story (probably apocryphal) about bassist Charles Mingus, who fired a trombone player who was widely considered the best player in his band. When a fan asked Mingus why he kicked out such a talented musician, Mingus replied, "Motherfucker never made any mistakes."

"Exactly!" Liu Yuan laughed, nodding. "That's our problem. We're taught from a young age to play correctly, like good little children. We've got to learn to break the rules. To be motherfuckers."

One striking characteristic of Chinese jazz musicians was their uniform reverence for Miles Davis. Almost to a person they preferred the spare, cooler style of Miles to the rapid pyrotechnic displays of other jazz artists. They pointed to his use of empty space and understatement, "saying more with less", all preferences that, it seemed to me, had a resonance with Chinese visual arts. The best selling jazz album of all time is Miles's classic *Kind of Blue*. In the liner notes to the album, pianist Bill Evans compared jazz improvisation to the art of calligraphy. I remember at the time thinking that it was a gratuitous comparison, a trendy invoking of Oriental exoticism. But it turned out my Chinese musician friends also saw commonalities in the two disciplines. The calligrapher, like the jazz artist, spends a lifetime mastering the basic forms in preparation for a spontaneous moment of creation, during which the artist must act in a non-deliberative way to produce one continuous, expressive "line" – for the calligrapher in space, for the jazz player in time – without the option of revising, restarting or rethinking. Each time the result is a unique form reflecting the artist's mental and emotional state at that moment. Miles's philosophy of jazz seemed to echo centuries of Chinese aesthetics. He famously told his sidemen, "Don't play what's there, play what's not there." If that's not Daoism, what is?

While there were several hotel jazz groups and sporadic jam sessions, the first real jazz gig in Beijing was at the San Wei Bookstore, an unassuming two-story structure just off of Chang'an Boulevard. The name was a reference to the school where Lu Xun studied as a child. The *san wei* or "three tastes" was a Qing dynasty term referring to the three important categories of books: history, poetry, and philosophy. Lu Xun and jazz – why not?

The owners, Liu Yuansheng and her husband Li Shiqiang, had converted the second floor into a traditional Chinese teahouse, with calligraphy scrolls on the wall and Qing-style furniture. The bookstore was popular with the Beijing intelligentsia, and also became a magnet for foreigners searching out some easily digestible Chinese culture. Even George HW Bush's vice-president Dan Quayle had sipped tea there during a visit to China. Liu and Li approached me with the idea of creating a jazz salon to introduce the music to a scholarly young audience.

"We know jazz is a great American art form," Liu Yuansheng told me. "We want to create an atmosphere where people come week after week and get to really understand the music, rather than just hearing snippets now and then."

It turned out to be not only the earliest but also the steadiest jazz gig in Beijing. Our group played nearly every Saturday for four years. The audiences were small but attentive, and I enjoyed the barrage of questions we received after. Puzzled by the long improvised solos, people asked me "How are you musicians able to memorize all those complicated melodies?" I told them that the music was completely ad-libbed, not memorized. "Well, without a score, how can you tell a wrong note from a right one?" Indeed. Or, "If the music is all improvised, then why bother to practice?" And, "How come the trumpet and saxophone all seem to take turns playing, while the drums, bass, and piano play all the time? They should be paid more!"

It was very satisfying to introduce jazz to young Chinese intelligentsia, but there was one annoying aspect to the performances. Someone in the audience would invariably request that we play Kenny G's "Going Home", under the impression that the curly-haired muzak saxophonist somehow represented the epitome of jazz art, based on his syrupy 1989 hit that went viral in China for a decade, and still can be heard in hotel elevators.

By the mid-90s, jazz in China was gaining momentum. Beijing got its first jazz festival, the brainchild of German expat Udo Hoffman. The Beijing Jazz Festival never really made money, but Udo's genius for procuring corporate sponsorship kept the annual event alive for many years, introducing audiences to Dave Holland, Paul Motian and legendary vocalist Betty Carter, who sang her last concert at the 1997 festival. Chinese jazz groups proliferated, and Beijing was on the verge of recreating the Shanghai jazz scene of the 1930s – without the opium and gambling. Crowds of curious young people showed up to listen, their fingers and toes gradually learning to tap to the swing rhythm on the second and fourth beat – the more "hip" way, as Duke Ellington observed – not on the first and third.

Local musicians now had the opportunity to meet and play with established foreign jazz stars. In the summer of 1994, after the Grammy-winning fusion-jazz group the Brecker Brothers performed to a sold-out crowd at Beijing's Poly Plaza, they showed up at our weekly jazz gig at a bar called Poacher's Inn, to check out local Chinese jazz. During the course of the night, they jammed with our group and the legendary Michael Brecker borrowed Du Yinjiao's tenor sax to play. Du was in ecstasy. "To think that Michael Brecker actually played my saxophone!" he said. "I'm going to take this reed off and frame it!" Then he added, "It probably has AIDS on it, anyway."

Around 1996, Du Yinjiao approached me with an idea. He wanted to recruit his PLA band buddies to form a traditional jazz big band, which would be the first of its kind since 1949. There were plenty of bored horn players stuck on the army base all day long, itching to play something more challenging and creative. All they needed was for me to arrange the musical charts.

The trickier problem was getting such a renegade ensemble approved by the PLA leadership. To the army upper echelons, jazz was a quintessentially degenerate style of music, closely associated with the KMT, prostitutes and Western decadence. Watch any Chinese revolutionary film from the 50s and 60s, and you'll find that scenes of *qipao*-clad harlots cavorting with slick-haired KMT spies in smoke-filled cabaret halls are invariably accompanied by cheesy jazz. Du did his best to convince the leadership of jazz's politically correct credentials. "Jazz should be championed by the Communist Party," he would tell them. "After all, it's music of the oppressed class, former black slaves of the land-owners!" But the army brass was unbending.

Nevertheless, we decided to forge ahead. I bought a dozen or so discount big band scores from the US, and we began rehearsals. The name chosen for the band was *Jinhaojiao Jueshi Yuedui*, "the Golden Horn Jazz Band". It turns out I was the first foreigner ever to come into the army band compound. When Du drove me to the rehearsal hall I had to duck down in the car so the guard at the checkpoint wouldn't see me. This subterfuge was met with great mirth by the band. "What military secrets are you going to steal," they teased me, "the chords to the Chinese national anthem?"

Rehearsals were chaotic at first. Many of the players had no idea what swing rhythm was all about, but slowly the band got the hang of it. Then a miracle happened. After amassing a repertoire of a dozen or so songs, they began to get gigs. Lots of them. It turns out that the foreign hotels were willing to pay good money to hire an honest-to-goodness jazz big band to play "Moonlight Serenade" in their ballrooms on New Year's Eve. At this point, the PLA generals, who heretofore had frowned on the endeavor, suddenly took a personal interest. Jazz could make money? Du Yinjiao promptly lost artistic control over the Golden Horn Jazz Band, but at least he was finally playing Benny Goodman.

Another fond memory is when Wynton Marsalis toured China with the Lincoln Center Jazz Orchestra. I was lucky enough to travel around with him and the group as a translator and bilingual host. Wynton was an inspiration, an evangelist for the jazz gospel, and audiences found him spellbinding. For me, translating for him was a constant improvised solo, providing on-the-spot translations for song titles like "East St. Louis Toodle-Oo" or "Goodbye, Porkpie Hat". The line that really stumped me was when during the Beijing master class Wynton quoted Duke Ellington: "I don't ask for perfection. All I ask for is goose pimples." An equivalent escaped me, but as I listened to a Chinese middle school boy navigate bebop changes on the alto sax with precocious assurance and verve, I felt it for the first time in China. Goose pimples.

Fast forward to 2012. It's a hot summer night, and I'm subbing for an ailing pianist at the East Shore Café, Beijing's premiere jazz club. The East Shore is co-owned by Liu Yuan, Cui Jian's saxophonist, who has converted to Buddhism and is in semi-retirement. Beijing now boasts some truly awesome jazz musicians—"monsters" in jazz parlance—who could occupy any international festival stage and make China proud. I myself feel lucky just to have a chance to occasionally play with some of these talents. My first friend in Beijing's jazz circles, Liang Heping, is not so lucky. He was paralyzed from the neck down in a freak car accident on a mountain road, and is confined to a wheelchair, unable to play a note on the piano. My PLA pal Du Yinjiao, meanwhile, has essentially given up jazz, and now spends his time teaching music and occasionally performing commercial music in concert halls to pay the bills.

During the break I go outside to the bank of Houhai lake with the drummer and bass player for some fresh air, swatting away mosquitoes. I can hear the faint background music from upstairs, Billie Holiday singing "You've Changed". It's one of her last recordings, and her is voice ravaged by years of drugs and alcohol as she sings:

You've changed

You're not the angel I once knew

I'm reminded about the changes that every jazz player must master, the changes that China must go through, the changes through which opposites give birth to cool and hot, freedom and constraint, East and West, all in search of the ultimate harmony spoken of in the original Book of Changes. The rest is just improvisation.

State of Media

Comic verse

———————————

Tom Fearon

I walked up to the gate of CCTV
in the summer of '09.
A soldier stretched his arm out,
his fingers reaching for mine.
He's friendly, I thought naively
And went to shake his hand,
But he pulled it back and said with a scowl:
"Show your ID, young foreign man!"

I sat before my computer,
its screen beckoned with a script,
a half-baked lede and awful blurb
in rich Chinglish did it drip.
I stripped it back to its bare bones
and gave some spit and shine,
it went to air minutes later
while I wrote the new headline.

Morning, evenings, overnights,
days melted into each other.
"Polish my story!" "Voice my sound bite!"
each request followed by another.

The job was simple, so it seemed,
for a native speaker who could spell.
They even supplied an oversized room
at the luxurious Friendship Hotel.

Sitting in the newsroom,
listening to James Chau
as he read the news from the studio
about a speech by Hu Jintao.
"Hurt feelings of the Chinese people"
he said in his best deadpan,
but nothing hurt quite as much
as another inedible *hefan*.

We got the graveyard shift
but some of us didn't mind,
sneaking out between newscasts
to roast a Zhongnanhai.
Minutes crawled like the news ticker,
sleeping at our desks 'til dawn
when others came to relieve us
with *baozi* and steamed corn.

An English-speaking cadre
was vigilant newsroom watchdog,
while a *laowai*-loathing nationalist
could host a show called *Dialogue*.
Behind the scenes, working hard,
toiled the talented young,
tomorrow's newsmen and women
quite unlike Rui Chenggang.

Media pals back home often asked
about life in the belly of the beast.
Wondering whether they
should also head out East.
It's not for all, that's for sure,
but you learn to adapt and stylize
when polishing another story
about boosting bilateral ties.

Two years went by in a flash
it had been a decent stint,
but something pulled me back toward
the familiar grasp of print.
Global Times was new on the scene
firing editorial barbs with spin,
headed by a mop-topped patriot
better known as Hu Xijin.

The pressure was higher than TV,
where news was shoveled out like coal
and a typo read out on the air
disappeared into a black hole.
But an extra space or missing comma
spells disaster in black and white.
All you can do is hope and pray
it evades your boss's sight.

But now it's time to stop the press
and end the journalism ride.
I've made some lasting friendships
and worked on stories with pride.
I'll miss the buzz of newsrooms,

dressing headlines with a pun,
but thanks for the memories, state media,
you've been a lot of fun.

Big in Beijing

Fiction

Carlos Ottery

FIRST AND FOREMOST Leroy considered himself a DJ. Sure, he wasn't averse to moonlighting as a language teacher for extra cash (after all, what was the point of speaking English if you couldn't spread the love a little, now and then?). That's what he loved about Beijing – the sheer variety of the work. There were so many great opportunities. Voice dubbing adverts, the film work — a speaking part was around the corner soon — and freelance editing. He wasn't polishing hotel brochures; he was doing actual *journalism*, writing for the trade publication *ChinAfrica*, which Robert Mugabe once described as "essential reading". But the DJing. Yeah, the DJing was Leroy's real passion.

In fact, Leroy was doing rather well for himself, pulling in about 7000 *kuai* a month from the Old Oriental Learning Centre alone. And his income could easily jump up to nine or even 13K when he factored in the DJing. Let's put it this way, Leroy had no problem getting a round of beers.

His long-term plan was to invest in some actual vinyl and get a few gigs with some of the hipper music collectives around town, perhaps Semiotic Sounds, Street Punks, or even The Acupressure Crew. His dream was to play at the famed White Lantern Club, but for the time being he was content to spin CDs at his Tuesday night residency at The Smuggler's Bar in Sanlitun.

Things were going pretty well there. He got 400 *kuai* per night and all the Tsingtaos he could drink. *City Weekend* called his night "eclectic, to say the least."

Leroy loved that. Imagine that, him, Leroy, in a magazine. "Eclectic, to say the least." That meant even more than eclectic. Leroy imagined himself playing a whole new sound to a packed out White Lantern. Soon the local papers would be calling him "post-eclectic". They would interview him in *Time Out*; one of the girls he was thinking about dating used to work there after all. Hell, they would probably give him some kind of column when they found out about his journalism, maybe with a picture of him at the top, behind his CD mixer, wearing a jaunty hat.

Back home in Norwich, there was no way he could be doing this sort of stuff, which, come to think of it, was probably why he had left. It's not that he didn't like Norwich; he had always felt right at home there. He had just somehow outgrown it all. He had wanted to do bigger things, to be a bit more of a man-of-the-world type. Back home, people didn't even know what *baijiu* was, and he often drank *baijiu* now. A lot of his foreign friends couldn't drink it, but Leroy was hardcore and just fitted in somehow. Beijing was his home now, and in Beijing he felt he was kind of a big deal.

And it wasn't just on the career front that things were taking off. Things were looking up on the lady front too. It was as though escaping England allowed him to escape from his past and from himself. He was freer here, more confident, and it undoubtedly showed with the ladies. He had, literally, dozens of numbers. Back home he had to work to get a girl's number, but here he would lay down the charm, tell a few jokes, then just ask, and the numbers would flow.

Back home Leroy was sick of the game, but in Beijing there was no game to be sick of. Girls accepted him for who he was.

They say the past is a foreign country, but Leroy knew that was all wrong. The future was a foreign country, and it was called China, the "Middle Kingdom".

And as for the women, bloody hell. Such beauties. Ya Ya, the receptionist from Old Oriental. Cherry, a student from the very same school. Bei Bei (he called her baby!) from Red Club; she couldn't speak English but was easily the most friendly girl of them all; he had even tried to kiss her once. Ting Ting from WeLovePeking.com, a really sweet social networking site for Beijingers. Leroy had almost had about five dates from that website alone. And there was Oogil, his language partner from Inner Mongolia. Leroy suspected he shouldn't date his language partner, but he had never had one for any length of time. Come to think of it, that was probably why he had never learnt the language. But he would in the future. No question about that.

All this meant going on dates about three or four nights a week, even if they weren't proper dates. Anyway, he would see them during his lessons, or one would come to his gig at The Smugglers and stand there, as Leroy, beaming, dropped classic track after classic eclectic track. Hip-hop, rock, dancy stuff – nothing was too out there for LeroyLeroy needed to focus on just one girl though. He was respectful. He wasn't a player and he didn't want to be. He respected women too much.

But things were going a bit slower than he liked, for all sorts of reasons. Chinese girls in Beijing were always looking to improve themselves. They were pretty career focused. Leroy, honestly speaking, was too much of a party animal for some of them. Besides, a lot of them didn't have time for a serious relationship. Ya Ya worked six days a week at Old Oriental. Cherry was really focused on her studies and setting up an English Corner. Leroy could always help on that front, he was a native English speaker after all, but he always missed the English corners – they were so early and often he had a headache in the morning. And Oogil had all her stuff going on at Maggie's bar, which meant she was busy most evenings.

The other problem was that Chinese girls were really traditional. They weren't like the women back home who would go to bed with anyone, well, with certain guys he knew at least. Chinese girls had a different culture. Sometime he took them out to the pub in the evening, and they would just have coffee. Leroy hated it when they did that. Why couldn't they just have a couple of beers like he did?

On the whole though, Leroy was completely fine with the cultural differences. He got China, and he got Beijing. He was genuinely down with it, unlike some foreigners who were just clueless. He knew that you had to take it slow with Chinese girls. It wasn't a big deal.

He had been doing a lot of stuff with these girls – watched a couple of movies, had quite a few hot pots, and walked around Chaoyang Park (three times). He'd even been to the Great Wall. He was on the cusp of something big and knew it.

His future flashed before him – the writing, the music, the Chinese wife, hell, he could easily open up a small bar or even his own language school. God, he loved this city. He was going to make it. And if that didn't work out, fuck it. He could always buy himself another Tsingtao.

AYI AND I
An unexpected friendship

Sam Duncan

I ARRIVED IN Daqing, a city in far northeast China famous for its oil fields, at the beginning of autumn when the nights were already approaching freezing point. I was employed by an "educational consultancy" firm to work as a foreign English teacher for a year in a local primary and middle school – basically a money-making scam. At the bus station I was met by Mike, a Chinese guy who had lived in Ireland for almost a decade and spoke English as fluently as a leprechaun and with the same accent.

On the cab ride to the school, oil pumps sped past while the sun set behind them in a sky full of billowing clouds. After three years in China I was excited to start a new job in a new city, and Mike excitedly told me about my apartment. "It's absolutely fabulous," he said in his lilting tones. "Massive, two bedrooms, the TV is a little old but it's a Sony and must have cost the owners more than 10,000 yuan. Grand it is."

When we arrived at the aging six-story walk-up, I soon realized it was the worst place I would ever spend a night in, let alone live in for a year. My apartment looked like it had been decorated by a deranged North Korean interior designer, with peach-colored plastic over the walls, industrially bright spotlights, dying plants in random corners and hundreds of children's stickers plastered everywhere. There was no hot water. The TV may well have cost a lot of money new, but it was 15 years old and broken. The kitchen was covered in grease and dirt. The bathroom was caked in mildew, mold, rust and dust. The single bed had a bare black-mold infested mattress on it that might have outdated the TV. The only decoration was a candle stuck in an empty Tsingtao beer bottle. The balcony had been used for food preparation, or perhaps for chopping up murder victims – there was blood splatter on the walls, and random yellowed bones with caked gristle on them that made the whole apartment smell like a kennel.

I resolved to move out the next day, and slept on the sofa the first night to avoid death by mold. I was woken by a knock on the door far too early in the morning, and when I opened it a large jovial man yelled "HELLO! I – AM – YOUR – LANDLORD" as clearly as he could in Chinese. When I answered in the same language, he visibly relaxed and shook my hand. Behind him was a woman with a perm wearing a bright pink sweater that declared in multi-colored lettering "I'M a Hip Hop STAR!! CUTES CAMPUS". She introduced herself as the landlord's mother, and they both invited themselves in, asking me if everything was okay. I told them the TV was broken and there was no hot water. My landlord, who was called Tiepeng (Iron Roc), told me he would install a new boiler for me later that day, and that the TV would work fine as soon as the housing contract was signed.

They soon noticed my bedding on the sofa, and the landlord's mother asked why I didn't sleep in the bed. I tactfully told her it was because I hadn't had time to clean the mattress yet. They disappeared into the bedroom for a minute and came out looking embarrassed. No worries, I said, everything is fine, but I might buy a new double bed anyway. They nodded and said that a double bed would definitely suit me better.

A couple of hours later there was another knock on the door, and a group of men walked in carrying a boiler and two single beds, accompanied by a grinning Tiepeng. I told him I didn't want the beds, that I would get my own, but he insisted. "My mother says she didn't know we were renting to a foreigner, and we need to welcome foreigners to our country. You can put these beds together to make a double." I didn't have a choice. Many cigarettes and lots of noise later, the beds were set up and the boiler tank installed, leaving the bathroom a mess of broken ceramic, burnt pipes and cigarette butts. Just when I started to clean up there was another rap at the door – five long, slow knocks, like Morse Code. I looked through the peephole and there was the landlord's mother, standing outside expectantly with a bowl of grapes.

She insisted I finish all the grapes in front of her, and asked me if they were good after every bite I took. We had the same conversation I've had with a thousand Chinese people before, but she seemed like a nice lady with a good sense of humor, and she wasn't patronizing or full of assumptions. Even in top-tier Chinese cities it can be hard to find older people who see past your foreignness and treat you like a human being. As we saw more of each other I felt grateful that she didn't pepper our chats with empty praise of my Chinese, my chopstick skills, or my ability to eat spicy food without choking to death. It was mostly because of her and her family's kindness that I decided to stay in the flat. She told me to call her Ayi – Auntie – and although she later told me her real name, I never used it and promptly forgot it.

Daqing is a city built on oil, and some residents like to compare it to Detroit. When the oil runs out, they say, the city will cease to exist. It was founded in 1959 and became a model industrial city, a household name throughout China. Located on what is essentially a sandy swamp, Daqing is extremely low density by Chinese standards, a deliberate measure to minimize losses in case of explosions. Oil pumps sit right next to bus stops and uninspiring apartment blocks. It is probably one of the ugliest cities in China, unless you like smokestacks and industrial parks.

Ayi and her husband had worked for one of the massive state-owned oil companies for most of their lives, before her husband passed away and Ayi retired. They had two apartments, both provided by their old company – they shared one, and Tiepeng had lived in the other with his young family before renting it out to me. While far from rich, Ayi collected two pensions and lived a comfortable life. Although she is one of the most giving and generous people I've ever met, she is still a product of her upbringing, and would happily spend a whole morning in a queue just to save a few cents on eggs.

I was their first tenant, and soon realized that she saw me as a boarder living in her spare room rather than as a stranger renting her property. She had knocked on the door opposite hers whenever she felt like it for the last 16 years, and she wasn't about to stop. I got used to her signature five-tap knock, which came without warning any time after 6am. She woke up at 5am herself, and walked to a construction site nearby where local farmers took their fresh produce on tractors and donkey carts to sell at lower prices than in the supermarkets. She returned home laden with vegetables and came across the hallway to see if I wanted any carrots, potatoes, eggplant, leek or whatever else was in season.

At first I tried to pretend I wasn't at home, but it never worked. She yelled, "I know you're home, I can see the light on!" If I shouted back that I was busy she might move on, but most of the time she just said "Open up, it's important!" When

I did she smiled and thrust a bag of sweet potatoes or onions into my hands. Refusal wasn't an option, because if I did refuse she just came back minutes later with an even greater choice of vegetables, and I didn't want to argue in the doorway.

At other times she needed my help. Ayi had a huge new flatscreen TV, and often got lost in the onscreen menus or turned the cable box off by mistake. She came knocking urgently so she wouldn't miss the nightly news at seven, or the Korean dramas afterwards. She had similar problems with her phone, and also needed a hand carrying bags of locally grown rice and Russian flour up the stairs.

The favors were always reciprocated, and I don't know what I would have done without her. Our complex had frequent water, power, heating and gas cuts, but Ayi always seemed to know exactly how long they would last, and who to call. If I went to the property management office with a complaint, they stalled and lied and refused to help – but if she went with me she nagged and yelled and browbeat them into submission, and before I knew it there would be a team of workers in blue overalls coming up to fix the problem.

One day I heard her knock as usual, and when I opened the door she rushed in with a stack of pink garbage pail buckets and told me to fill them up with water from the kitchen immediately. When I asked why she forced another pail into my hands and told me to fill that one from the bathroom tap. I kept asking why until finally she looked at me like I was a complete moron. "The water will be cut off any moment now," she said, "for two days. You'll need this water to flush the toilet, clean, shower and cook." She was right, of course, and if I didn't have that water it would have been a nasty couple of days.

As time went by we fell into a routine. Ayi learned to leave me alone in the mornings, unless it was a grocery emergency, and in the evenings she brought over fruit or a snack of some kind, and we sat and chatted for a while. Sometimes we argued about issues like Sino-Japanese relations. Her family, like so many all over China, were rabidly anti-Japanese, and she almost always used terms like "little Japanese" and "Japanese devils" to describe the people. Years ago I used to laugh along blithely when people made such horrible racist statements, but nowadays I try to present an alternative viewpoint. Sometimes I got irritated and said I had work to do; sometimes she did the same and stormed out. The next day it was always forgotten.

I was interested in her early life and asked a lot of questions, and she would answer happily but never talk about anything too private. On the evening Nelson Mandela died, in December 2013, Ayi invited me into her flat to watch the news. As the tributes rolled in I got a little emotional. Maybe it was seeing me tear up over Mandela, but that night Ayi started to talk about the Cultural Revolution, and from then on it became one of her favorite topics. Over the weeks and months she told me dozens of stories about her life and family history. No one else was interested, she told me. Her sons never asked about it, her friends and relatives didn't talk about it, and her husband was gone.

Ayi was born in the port city of Tianjin in the mid 1950s, but her extended family moved to Harbin, provincial capital in the Northeast, soon after she was born. Her father's family were landowners and involved in commerce of some kind. She described how her paternal grandmother could use an abacus with each hand doing different sums, a skill she passed on to her own sons and daughters. But her family on her mother's side were uncultured peasants. Ayi barely talked about them, and when she did it was dismissively.

Ayi often lamented that she never went to university. When the Cultural Revolution started in 1966, she was in the third year of middle school, and most of her teachers were sent away, some never to be heard from again. She said it was a great shame that so many cultured people lost their jobs, while their replacements were useless. Soon afterwards the universities closed, and with them went any hope of becoming an educated woman. Her family was relatively well-off, but since most people in the Northeast at that time were relatively new arrivals, there wasn't the same animosity towards landlords as existed in other areas of the country.

Even still, her family had all of its land and wealth confiscated in the Cultural Revolution. That included books, clothes, family heirlooms, memorial tablets, anything of value. Everything old was lost, and they counted themselves lucky that they weren't beaten. Among the confiscated property was her family tree, a cloth banner they hung on the wall every Spring Festival. On it were written the names of all her ancestors going back generations, as well as instructions on how to name future male descendants. The women's given names were unrecorded, simply listed as "wife" under their husband's surname. Her grandmother had tried to hide the precious heirloom in the attic, but the authorities had found it and taken it away. When Ayi was young, she and the other girls had been given the task of memorizing it, but they were too busy playing to bother. Now the names are lost forever.

But Ayi also has fond memories of the Cultural Revolution. There was a strong community spirit, with communal dining halls and free buses. Even though they were dirt poor, no-one minded because everyone was in the same situation. Once things calmed down and it was safe to make money again, her father cooked trays of tofu and sold it on the street. From the profits he built a new business, and soon her family had money again. She told me this story several times, and regarded it as concrete evidence that her family was innately predisposed to education and wealth. The way she saw it, although the Cultural Revolution made everyone equal for a while, when the restrictions were lifted the capable families reclaimed their rightful places at the top of the pile.

All the while, Ayi was in touch with an old high school classmate who had joined the military. He was posted in Daqing, and they wrote each other letters. In one letter he asked her to come and see him. She knew what that meant, and months later they were married. I asked if they had been in a relationship during high school, but she insisted that no one had thought about that kind of thing back then – romances between secondary school students were unheard of. I pushed further, suggesting there must have been some kind of feeling between them, but she denied it. She said, simply, that it was a different time.

I learned a lot from Ayi in my year in Daqing, and not just about history. If I had let her she would have made me breakfast, lunch and dinner every day, and cleaned my apartment too. It seemed like she spent every waking hour either buying vegetables or turning them into food for her son's family. She made me literally thousands of dumplings, that she would bag up and stuff in my freezer, and every time a relative slaughtered a pig and sent her the meat she would give me a cut. On holidays I was invited to eat and drink with the extended family, and at Spring Festival they bought me couplets to hang on my door, and lucky red paper cuttings for the windows. They never asked for anything in return.

Ayi fretted over the fact that I was single and unmarried in my thirties, and constantly offered to arrange a marriage for me.

She harassed me about having a child as soon as I could, "to make your mother happy." Tiepeng, meanwhile, was the perfect example of a filial son. He worked long hours in the oilfields for low pay – the first meal we had together he told me he was in charge of safety, but I later found out he was a security guard. This didn't stop him from visiting his mother daily, no matter how busy he was, while my parents were lucky to get an email once a week, or a monthly Skype call.

Ayi cried when I left Daqing in the autumn of 2014. I promised to write, but haven't yet. Maybe writing this will motivate me to send her a long-overdue letter. Meanwhile, I'm sure she still bores her plaza-dancing friends with stories about the stubborn foreigner who refused to wear thermal underwear, drank cold water all year round and overcooked his dumplings.

Mid-Autumn Lanterns

A sonnet

Rosalyn Shih

Drinking soft flame and light, the lantern swells
with heat that beats against its paper walls,
burning my fingertips until, released,
it sails into the stillness of the night.
I remember that sweating summer day
we breathed each other in, and sighing out,
I felt my paraffin chest expand with
the same fragile warmth of a wish lantern.
On a Guangzhou rooftop, now, I look up.
Faith, guide me this vessel to sail across
the Lingnan plains and the South China Sea;
though miles apart, we share the same full moon.
Love, perfect for me this diaphanous heart
that waxes and wanes, but ever beating still.

The Cornfield Grave

Paying last respects

Carl Setzer

"42, 43, 44, 45. I think this is the spot."

Grandpa stopped and searched for his cigarettes, trying to ignore the pain in his hands and legs.

"When I was a boy it was 45 paces from the farmhouse," he continued. "I think that building is the original structure. It was located in the back corner of the third lot from County Lane 62. That has to be it. But nothing looks familiar anymore."

It had been many years since his oldest son had passed away, and time had changed the landscape.

Grandpa, my wife and I stood together, watched over by the curious stares of a handful of local farmers. It must have been an odd National Day holiday for them, witnessing our impromptu memorial ceremony. The presence of three strangers in the middle of a cornfield was strange enough. That one of them was a large foreigner must have been simply baffling.

"This has to be the first time a foreign devil has been to this part of China," one of the farmers whispered.

The foreign devil didn't feel out of place, though. I had been preparing for this journey for a long time, perhaps a lifetime. The field, the farmhouse and the farmers all seemed to be part of a distant reality for me. My mind, for the moment, was focused on the emotions of Grandpa and my wife.

"Look over there!" Grandpa said to my wife. "If that corner was where my mother was buried, your father was only two places away to the left." The October ground was covered in rows of last year's dried corn stalks, and Grandpa sidestepped over them, trying not to stumble.

"At least they didn't grow crops in this field this year," he mumbled.

"When did the government take this land from us, Grandpa?" my wife asked, as we walked.

"The government didn't take this land from us, my girl. We never owned it. When they removed our grave markers and served us with the notices, the government merely reminded us that it was never ours.

"How long ago was that?"

She had got used to her grandfather's manner when she was a young girl, and it still influenced the way they talked. She knew his contempt for the Party could only be expressed in blunt, sardonic statements.

"It has been fifteen years since the government was gracious enough to remind us that we didn't own it," he replied. "It's the land of the people, but not of our people."

When we arrived at the spot Grandpa had led us to, my wife waited attentively with the eight lilies she had bought for the occasion. "Six white and two pink," she said to no one in particular.

Grandpa responded with a grunt. The farmers seemed to have lost interest and went back to smoking cigarettes and chatting. My mind wandered for a minute to ponder the question of whether they knew what existed on this land, below their cornhusks and cigarette butts. I decided that they probably didn't, and that it would be in vain to try and explain.

A gentle wind blew. Grandpa and my wife thought that

this was as good a place as any. Whatever ashes were interned under this soil had long since nourished several seasons of crops, dissipating across the field. In a sense, whether or not we were in the exact spot didn't matter. We had come to pay homage to a soul not forgotten, and this ceremony was only a small part of what we felt inside.

My wife laid down the bouquet of flowers, ribbons facing west. Then she paused for a second, and turned them to face the east. She leaned into my chest and faced the makeshift grave, tears streaming down her face. I tried to wipe mine away as well, but for each one I caught, two more fell to the dusty earth.

I finally let go of her, and she dried her own tears. She knelt down, straightened the ribbons, and began to speak.

"I came to see you, Dad. I brought my husband and your father. We are all here and everyone is healthy. I'm sorry I didn't bring my husband to meet you before the wedding. I'm so embarrassed, but we are here now. He's a good man, I love him and he loves me. He's given me a good home and he protects my heart. You would like him, Dad."

She fell silent for a while, then prayed for good fortune and peace for her father in the next life. She got up, dusted off the dirt from her knees and returned to my arms. I watched how the petals of the lilies moved with the wind, and a sharp pang shot through my heart like a knife. I knew that at that moment, none of us would choose to be anywhere else.

Grandpa turned and faced the resting place of his son, a life taken too soon. He drew a cigarette from the pack, lit it, took a long slow drag and then placed the cigarette at the base of what might have been the grave of his son.

Smoke rose up into the wind. A gust caught the cigarette and rolled it gently into a groove of corn stalk, where it rested, smoldering. I broke down again at the brevity of the gesture and layers of emotion behind it. A grandfather robbed of a son, a daughter deprived of her father, and a husband without a hero.

"Son, I'm sorry I didn't bring my daughter and her husband here earlier. We should have brought him to meet you before the wedding. I'm so embarrassed. But don't worry about her, my boy, she is going to be fine. She found a man that loves her and they are happy."

Grandpa's strong voice broke as the years of pain and sadness came back to him. He continued, weeping.

"She has a good job and a warm home. They will give you grandchildren one day and our name will live on. We didn't bring you anything today, just these flowers. It's not the festival of the dead, so you can stay here and rest. We just wanted to introduce you to the man who married your daughter."

I looked down, and saw that the wind had smoked more of the cigarette. The three of us stood in silence for a moment, waiting for the tears to subside.

"I could never find this place again," my wife said.

I helped Grandpa to step over an irrigation trench as we returned up the pathway. Along the way, I counted the steps.

"95 steps, my love, third field on the right from County Lane 62," I told my wife. She responded with a forced smile. Then she asked quietly: "Can we bring our kids here one day?"

"Of course we can."

DUMPLINGS

A short story

Michael Salmon

ANOTHER MEAL TOGETHER. They couldn't simply spend the evenings ignoring each other. Gary still wanted to complain a little.

"Why don't we find a new place, outside the complex? I'm starting to feel like I'm living in a fortress. Let's go somewhere out on the streets, you know?"

"Fine," his cousin replied. "I know a good place."

They walked to the back of Charlie's apartment block, around the high metal fence you couldn't see through. The buildings dropped in height and grew darker, and the streetlights changed color, orange instead of white. Charlie suggested they take the bus a couple of stops, but Gary just wanted to be outside and see Beijing's back alleys, roads he had never been down in the two weeks he'd already spent as his cousin's lodger.

An arrangement made under duress, it seemed. Charlie had lived in Beijing for six or seven years, as far as Gary knew, teaching and translating, keeping to himself. But it wasn't as if Gary couldn't fend for himself; he had been round various parts of the country on holidays before, even lived in Shanghai for a few months. Not enough to impress his reluctant host, however. Charlie looked down on his scarce Chinese and, well, his enthusiasm, was it?

They walked by houses with tumbling slate roofs and drawn

blinds, an occasional newsagent, tobacconist or sex shop dotted between. The primary schools and health centers were already locked for the night. Night watchmen sat alone in illuminated booths, reading newspapers or else staring out into the street, gauging the night for trouble. None seemed likely to come; the streets were quiet save for the buzzing of scooters in the distance, always a few roads farther on.

The area was neither poor nor rich, Gary thought. He kept recording details, the rare signs of movement and life while Charlie walked a stride or two ahead, quiet and straight.

After fifteen minutes walking they emerged on a main road. Here, suddenly, people conglomerated and burst across roads without traffic lights; taxis dropped off and picked up; the pavement had small areas for sport, exercise, and outdoor seating. The air smelled fresh and damp, as if water was nearby, some low canal going green with weeds and algae.

Most importantly of all, hundreds of places to eat – by far the majority of the shops were restaurants or window stalls for takeaway. Gary and Charlie turned left and brushed by the entrances, waiters running in and out, and they could see food on tables, bright dishes, rice bowls, tea pots in the more expensive places, metal cylinders full of wooden chopsticks in the cheap ones, yellow-walled, crowded, paper table coverings, dirt on the floor, meat on racks, cigarettes steaming, kitchens open, the walls adorned with calligraphy and pictures of farm animals and menus all in Chinese characters. Each restaurant seemed in the middle of a celebration.

Gary asked his cousin why he hadn't brought him here before. He didn't get a clear answer.

"You see that place with the *jiaozi* sign?" Charlie shouted over the noise. "That's where we should go."

"What sign, where?"

"The red one, that one."

Inside, the restaurant was cloudy with condensation – wet ceiling and walls, trickling down and being mopped up by paper towels all along the windowsill. Every dish was served too hot to touch and still soaked with steamer water, bursting out with mist every time one of the couples or family groups who surrounded them picked up a dumpling and bit into it, panting from the temperature and then laughing together. Gary smiled at this too, looking at the wall displays of immaculately photographed dumplings, trying to spin his chopsticks on his fingers, holding up and sniffing the vinegar bottles.

Charlie looked uncertain, awkward in this new, different environment. When the waiter approached, he spoke with the fewest words possible. This is what I want.

Gary insisted they try a whole bunch of different kinds even though Charlie said three *jin* would be way too much food. It would be a bad idea.

If I could speak Chinese like that, I'd do it all the time, Gary thought. Ask people how's life, how's business. What was the point of this reluctance to fit in, this refusal to enjoy being in China?

"Hey, see what I've got," Gary said as they waited. He took out a tiny plastic container from his jacket pocket – a Chinese chessboard. It was a travel set, with a creased plastic sheet which had the grid lightly printed on top.

"Cool, huh? I bought it last weekend. It was only three *kuai*. Playing back in the apartment is fine, but really we should be playing outside, like the Chinese do." Charlie looked doubtful. "Come on, you don't want a rematch before the food arrives? I'll give you a decent game this time."

"Um, that's ok."

"Why not?"

His cousin shifted in his seat on the other side of the table. "It just seems like…drawing attention. There might not be time."

"What's the worst that could happen?" Gary asked, annoyed suddenly.

"People will see it as some kind of statement, I don't know. I'm not trying to say—"

"So, someone might come over and speak to us, is that what you're afraid of? Mate, we live here."

"Speak to *us*?" Both of their tones had quickly changed. "They're not going to speak to you, are they? It'll be me that has to speak."

"Oh, for fuck's sake, fine." Gary started to put the set away, and then stopped and left it on the side of table, unopened but visible through its clouded plastic case. The food arrived, and the waiter put the three bowls piled with dumplings down in the middle, the potential playing-area gone.

Gary laughed without humor. "You're right, we ordered too much."

They didn't speak as they ate. Gary worked through the *jiaozi* without looking up, too fast, wanting to finish them all, to get the meal over with and to prove he hadn't been wrong. His insides were heavy, and steam came from every mouthful.

When he looked up at Charlie, he saw blood trickling out of his cousin's nose, on his septum, trickling off to one side of his lips. He was still chewing, not realizing what had happened. Gary pointed, and at that moment Charlie must have felt it – the awareness made it suddenly stream. Fat red drops splattered the table.

"Shit." Charlie grabbed a napkin and held it to his nose, and it immediately turned red. "It's the heat, it's too hot." Heads turned towards them. One of the serving staff ran over, and Charlie spoke fast. His accent sounded snarling, more like the true Beijing rasp. Gary still hadn't moved or said anything. "Pay the bill," his cousin said. "The toilet's outside somewhere."

Charlie's chair clattered over as he raced for the door outside. Gary realized he still had food in his mouth, unable to swallow. And then he relaxed and asked for the *mai dan*, and the man nodded and strode off. Blood had spread across the paper tablecloth.

The waiter came back and said something. Gary sat mute. The man gestured to ask if Gary wanted the leftovers packed up to take away. They still had a plate-and-a-half untouched. He felt too bloated to even think about it. "*Bu yao, chi bao le*," he said, pleased to remember the expression. I'm full. The man picked up the plates and gave him a look: what does being full have anything to do with it? But Gary didn't want to eat these things again anytime soon. He left the money neatly on the table. Then his mobile rang. It was Charlie. "Bring some napkins," he said. "There's no paper here. It's on the right."

Gary pulled a dozen from the dispenser on the table, pocketed them, and left. He couldn't see Charlie anywhere. He turned right up a narrow alley, but there was no toilet, no sign for a toilet. More boarded-up windows and doors with peeling paint, single front steps that took up half the width of the passage. The buildings were either half-made or half-collapsed, missing bricks from walls and dead quiet with people sleeping inside, air ebbing in and out. No lights until the furthest point. He headed towards its glow, stepping around food bones and smashed up fruit. The ground felt hot.

At the end was a green curtained doorway, the same material for restaurant entrances and old men's coats, the quilted, plasticky tank-green that came out in the winter.

"Charlie?" he called.

"In here," came the voice.

Behind the fabric was his cousin, head inclined to keep it from touching the filthy ceiling. He was letting his nose run into the public toilet's hole, which looked like a swimming pool foot-wash, a step down into liquid, except for the brown shit and vegetable scraps, and a vertical streak of black blood on the surface.

"Take them," Gary said, thrusting the napkins into Charlie's damp hand. An electric light buzzed above them that seemed too bright, or maybe it was only that Gary had just stepped in from the night. There was barely room for both of them to stand on the surface above the pit, squashed together at one end of the stinking room. It was hard for Gary to inhale without his diaphragm lurching. Mosquitoes whined around his ears.

"I'll leave you to it, shall I?" Gary stepped back outside. He took a few deep breaths and calmed down.

He felt an impulse to record some details of a place like this. You needed to appreciate it, not just turn up your nose. He took out his phone and began taking photos – the peeling stickers on the doors, the smudged food on the ground, the alley with its tips of corrugated iron. When he looked around again he saw Charlie staring right at him from the doorway.

His cousin seemed disgusted at the presence of the phone, which Gary didn't understand. Why would you judge me for taking a few photos? Gary wanted to ask. Where was the harm in that? And yet Gary still felt like he'd been caught doing something wrong.

"Listen, mate. It wasn't like I was going to ask you to take one of me."

It was meant as a joke, but Charlie simply held out his hand for the phone. Gary handed it over without thinking, surprised by the gesture.

In one motion, Charlie swept back through the curtain and

threw the phone into the toilet pit. It slid under the surface and was gone.

Gary looked on aghast. For a moment, he was too shocked to say anything. What had he done to offend? Was Charlie afraid the locals would think he was looking down on them somehow? Who was Charlie to take offense on others' behalf, anyway? Did he think he was one of them?

"Nobody was going to see. There's no-one watching." It was an apology.

Charlie shrugged. "Now you have something to write about on Facebook."

And then Gary was shouting abuse at a retreating figure. His cousin was striding back down the alley, disappearing into the dark.

At the main road, catching up: "What the fuck is wrong with you?"

Charlie ignored him completely. "I suppose you know which bus to take home? Or should I lead the way again?" he finally said.

When the bus pulled up, there was nothing to do but be swept on by the crowd. Charlie took the one seat that was available, holding the red and white paper towels like a face mask, staring out the window or, no doubt, watching the reflection of the faces looking at him from behind. Gary stood in the aisle and rocked with the motion of the vehicle.

LIFE IS AN INTERNET CAFÉ

Intersecting strangers

Cobus Block

I MET HER on a crosswalk in Yiwu, a city in eastern China best known for trinket trade and socks sold by the container. The traffic was thick and we were both stranded together between lanes. As I searched down the street for a gap in the oncoming vehicles, I noticed she was watching me. She caught my eye and, instead of looking away, smirked and shook her head.

"It's crowded," I broke the ice.

Most Chinese outside the main cities are taken aback when they hear a foreigner speaking their language. She only shrugged her shoulders and responded, "It could be worse."

I laughed in agreement. She continued to look at me, but made no attempts to pursue the conversation. I saw a space between two small cars and stepped into the lane.

"Where are you going?" she asked as she moved in beside me.

I drew up short of a passing vehicle, moved around a motorcycle and replied over my shoulder, "I'm not sure, I just got here. What about you? Where are you going?"

"That way," she pointed down the street to her right.

I reached the curb and slowed my pace.

"Where are you going?" she asked again.

"I really don't know. I'm just looking around. Is there anything good to see in this town?"

"Nope."

I laughed at her terseness. "Well, what are you doing?"

"I already told you, I'm going that way."

"What's that way?"

She gave me a strange look.

"I mean," I said as I moved forward to allow an electric scooter around me, "Why are you going that way? Where are you going? Your home? A job? Somewhere else?"

"No. It's a park, and it has a lot of people."

I did not understand the attraction of a park with lots of people, but I had been honest when I told her I did not know why I was in Yiwu. At the time I was studying Chinese in the nearby city of Hangzhou. In my eyes, everything about China was new and fascinating. I was eager to learn, to meet people, to see as much as I could. My enthusiasm, coupled with the warm spring weather, made classes increasingly unbearable, until one day I grabbed my jacket and passport and ran to the bus station. Something about the name Yiwu — which I translated in my head as "righteous crow" — appealed to me, and I boarded the first bus bound in that direction.

"Well, may I come with you?" I asked. I decided I would rather go to a crowded park with company than stand on a crowded street with none.

She shrugged her shoulders and nodded.

As we walked we exchanged introductions. She was small, but something about her gait made her seem formidable. More than once she snapped at vendors and beggars trying to hustle the passing foreigner. In a voice too rough for someone only 23 years-old she told me her name was Yang. She was living with her brother in Yiwu while working for a company involved in international trade. What exactly her job entailed, she never said.

At first I had some difficulty understanding her strong Jiangxi accent, but she spoke slowly and deliberately, which made the conversation easy to follow.

After a few minutes of walking, we arrived at an open space with a few trees, winding sidewalks and sprinkled benches. This, she announced, was the park. It was full of boisterous young people and hawkers, and did not look very appealing.

I spotted a row of hotels across the street and said I should find a room for the night. She shook her head and told me those were bad hotels, I should just sleep in a *wangba*, one of China's less than sanitary Internet cafés. The name literally translates as "net bar"—which is remarkably appropriate, as they have a knack for combining the worst attributes of both the Internet and a bar. I thought I could get a cheap room at one of the smaller hotels, which would be more comfortable.

"No," she said in English, "no good," then explained that those hotels were for "bad" things. I must have looked confused, because she clarified.

"Whores," she pronounced with severity. "*Jinü*. No good."

"They are all just for prostitutes?" I asked incredulously.

She nodded her head, "Why not just spend the night in a *wangba*? You can chat with some people for a while, watch movies …"

"But it's too loud," I protested.

"No, no. There are a lot of people, but they won't bother you."

She saw I was unconvinced and promised to help me find a "good" hotel. I thanked her and asked if she would first like to get something to eat. She agreed, and we walked down the street away from the park. In one of the nearby alleys, we found a dumpling stand. As we sat down to eat, she began to tell me her story.

Yang came to Yiwu a year before after a stint in her hometown of Changnan, Jiangxi, where she lived with her widowed mother. When her mother passed away, Yang left to find her brother in Yiwu. I asked her where she had lived before returning to Changnan. Had she been studying? Working? She shook her head in response to both questions. She spent five years living in Zhejiang's coastal city Taizhou, she said, with her ex-husband.

"I was married to him when I was 15," she explained, "My brother was in school then, my father had been killed in a knife fight, and my family didn't have enough money to support everyone. His family did, and he was in business. I married him to support my mother and brother."

"When you were 15?" I asked. "Isn't that illegal?"

She smiled, "Things can be arranged."

"Why did you divorce?"

"Because he was a stupid cunt!" she snorted and then laughed when she saw I understood the obscenity, "He had no feelings, nothing. I had learned all I needed to know from him, so I left."

She started to hum a melody as she lifted a dumpling and dunked it in a bowl of vinegar and chili paste.

"So it was you who decided to get divorced, not your husband?"

"Me," she confirmed as she finished the dumpling, "Is my getting a divorce bad?"

"No, who says it's bad? I'm just curious."

"Curious? Why are you curious?" She stopped eating. "Chinese divorces are not easy. Once you're divorced, there's no money, no food, no relatives. It's the same as being a dead person. People stay married even if they have no feelings for each other, because it's more difficult to be divorced." She let her words sink in before reaching for another dumpling.

"Plus," she added with a shrug, "it's hard for my daughter."

"Your daughter? You have a daughter?"

"She doesn't like it," she sighed.

"Where is she now?"

"My in-laws took her."

"Do you go to visit her?"

"No. I can't."

"You can't see your daughter?"

"I can. If I wanted to, I could go see her everyday, that's the law. But it's hard for her, and I don't have any reason to see her."

"So, how many times have you seen her?"

"Three times."

My eyes widened, "How old is she?"

"Six."

I was stunned into silence for a moment.

"My brother has no baby," she said, trying to change the topic.

"But your daughter," I said, unwilling to let the topic go even though I knew I was imposing. "I think you should go see her more often."

She shook her head defensively and leaned in to ensure I understood her, "I want to have a career. I have my own life, my own affairs. If I use all my money to go see her, will I have money later? Will I be able to support others? I have to do it this way even if I want to see her."

She broke off and leaned back into her chair. After a moment's pause she continued in a tone that carried a tinge of pleading, "At that time I was just a teenager. If you give a little girl in marriage, she doesn't understand anything."

I couldn't think of any words that would be appropriate, so instead I took another dumpling and concentrated on chewing. When we finished our meal, Yang put her elbows on the table and rested her chin in her hands.

I put down my chopsticks and broke the silence, "So, will you get married again?"

"No. I'll just live as one person. I don't want to get married."

"Already tried that, huh?" I asked as I stood and produced my wallet.

She laughed, "Yeah, it was a disappointment."

I never discovered whether the hotels in Yiwu were dens of prostitution, as Yang claimed. None of the cheaper options would board a foreigner, and I had no money to pay for an expensive room. That night I slept in a *wangba*. It was hot and stuffy, and for a long while I couldn't sleep. Across the row from me a young man smoked a cigarette and pounded away furiously at his keyboard. In front of him two teenage girls typed instant messages to their friends, who might have been thousands of miles away or at a terminal across the room. On the wall a poster advertised a world where everyone can be a hero.

As I gazed across the room, full of faces focused intently on their screens, I remembered what Yang had told me earlier. "Life is like an internet café," she said, "You can chat with anybody you want. Sometimes you find an old friend, sometimes you find a new one, but in the end you're still alone."

NURSERY RHYME FOR BEIJING

Poetry

Canaan Morse

Rain, rain start to fall,
wash the window-studded walls.
Through the sewers thread your way,
flush the oil out to sea.

Rain, rain pouring down,
blessing for this desert town,
boiling in its crowded squares,
lost amid our blind desires.

Rain, rain please don't go;
through your glass we see our foe;
black his car and black his shoes,
in his pocket all the keys.

Rain, rain come again,
clear the noise and bare the skin.
Green the leaf, and nurse the tree.
Give us leave to see the sky.

December 2012, Beijing. AQI: 384

SHOWER BUSINESS

Last days of a Beijing bathhouse

Robert Foyle Hunwick

HONG SHENG, *qigong* master, can perform nude splits on a bridge of cracked tiles in a room the temperature of Mount Doom like a man half his age. That's how some guys like to roll in China: the backslapping, the *baijiu* toasting, the bonobo displays of power. Beijing's last old-style bathhouse isn't the kind of place to worry about stray hairs, clean towels or a brace of someone else's overripe cherries.

Just shy of a century old, the Shuangxingtang bathhouses in the far south Beijing suburb of Fengtai is one of the capital's toughest buildings, having (so far) survived a republic, various warlords, a full-scale occupation and a bitter civil war, followed by everything the Communist Party could throw at it. It's fitting that property developers are most likely to finish this place off. A shame – there aren't many hideaways where one can escape from decorum so cheaply. Napping, grumbling, smoking and masculine displays are all being pushed out to the suburbs.

Don't expect, or wish for, much courtesy from the older generation at Shuangxingtang (established 1916). They've had it with the outside world and its highfalutin ways, and this is their last-chance saloon. Next door to my booth, on arrival, some used long johns were draped over the shared divide. I had assumed that they belonged to the gentleman dozing in the adjoining stall and ignored the pair, like you would any old man's underwear. Sensing my presence, he jerked to attention and looked straight at the soiled drawers. "Get this crap out of my face!" he barked.

It turned out he was talking to someone behind me: 'Little Kim', barely a day over twelve and in charge of shoveling these old bastards' shit. Already he bore the look of a portly North Korean dictator, and the thin sheen of exertion on his moon-like face spoke of purges to come. Some day, I consider, this Kim will make an upstanding official or truculent businessman. Or if it goes wrong for him, maybe a career janitor.

That isn't odd anymore to me, to see an adolescent gofer serving far older, possibly wiser, undeniably more wizened men. This was how the public baths of Rome might have looked in their dingier sections, reserved for the hoi polloi, away from the sophisticated symposia: Down Fengtai, rather than up Pompeii. It turned out I was wrong about Kim – the sly fellow was 17, or that's what he claimed, enthusiastically smoking on a gold-tipped Hongsha. Despite the obligatory 'No Smoking' signs, hunkering down with a brightly colored cigarette is a cherished pastime at Shuangxingtang.

While bathhouse culture still thrive in China, the model is changing in the big cities. Back when indoor plumbing was a luxury, your grandfather might say "the rich go to the doctor and the poor visit a bathhouse." They were an essential part of the community: people gathering to eat, smoke, sleep, argue, play Chinese chess, sleep, watch cricket fights, smoke, eat, sleep, read the latest tabloid insights, drink, smoke, eat and sleep, all while telling their family they were just popping out for a communal bath. Now the rich are visiting bathhouses in droves, and favor the deluxe rub to the plebeian tub.

Big bathhouses these days are expected at the least to have

some upstairs massage rooms, with special services, rotating buffets and flatscreen televisions showing sports. Sweating in the nude, next to a shrewd investor, crooked cadre or blubbery cop, comrades are all rendered equal (there's less risk of being recorded and blackmailed afterward, too). It costs over two hundred yuan to visit one of new-fangled bathhouses – where hot-spring pools are decked out with fake trees, ornate footbridges, uniformed attendants and fish that nibble at your dead skin – and less than ten yuan to get the full Monty at historic joints like Shuangxingtang.

It's not just the lifestyle that is dying here – it's the customers. Places like Shuangxingtang are literally running out of punters. In September 2014, the Xinyuan baths in Haidian district, allegedly built under the Guangxu Emperor, had their doors closed for them by a bulldozer. Well-intentioned local regulations, designed to keep the facilities affordable, had prevented Xinyuan and places like it from increasing their fees enough to pay the rising bills, consigning the business to history.

The Xiong family, who have owned Shuangxingtang for the last two decades, know their shop has its name writ in water. The walls are speckled with evidence of a losing battle with mildew, where the forces of ayi and her mop-bucket are in retreat. Most tiles are cracked or missing around the larger tubs, and the grouting has a giddy, mustard tan that speaks to years of nicotine fug. Shuangxingtang was the main shooting location for the film *Shower*, which received multiple international awards and "two thumbs up!" from Roger Ebert in 1999. That was 16 years go and all attempts made on the back of the film to apply for World Intangible Cultural Heritage status have failed. The place is doomed, and I can't explain why.

There are huge, blown-up photographs depicting key scenes from *Shower* braving every room (I initially mistook them as adverts for the services offered). These are misleading if it's spa facilities you're after. Seek out a creamy facial mask, or a soothing peel, and you'll be met with a polite stare – this is your great-grandfather's grandfather's kind of place, no fuss and most certainly no muss. There's supposedly a KTV upstairs, but I didn't dare risk it.

Other than that Mandopop upstairs, not much seems to have changed since the Cultural Revolution. There are still framed, black and white photographs of Mao Zedong and Lin Biao hanging in the changing room, although they're kept well apart, at opposite ends, in fact, with Mao on the left and Lin on the right – politically correct even in death. Thirty years on, Lin Biao remains the PRC's foremost traitor and public enemy, so to display his portrait takes indignance, indifference or some merry prankster at work. It's especially ironic in this context, as he was supposedly terrified of water.

It was past dusk on a chilly winter's evening when my companion Jay and I groped our way through the neighborhood, searching for the right bathhouse among an array of identical, dimly lit alleys. It was six o'clock, so naturally the street was deserted, and there was no one to tell us where we were, nor any landmarks – just row upon row of dingy shops, restaurants and lock-ups selling hubcaps and other motoring goods, plus the occasional, evil-looking karaoke joint. We watched a depressed-looking 30-something hostess in a down coat begin her shift at an ominous Entertainment Complex offering "Massage, Sauna, KTV", and hoped to God this wasn't the place. It wasn't: we had passed it a block back.

Entrance was a cool eight yuan. For another twenty, they throw in a full rubdown (recommended) along with the complete day of soaking. No overnighters, a sign warns – they've had trouble with those, and besides, there's a hotel next door. Shuangxingtang doesn't see a lot of trade from foreigners and we got the traditional bathhouse welcome: a friendly nod, then an unbridled stare downward. Whether it's a glance or a glare, other customers rarely hid their curiosity and I chided myself for not offering better entertainment – an elaborate green merkin or 'Drink Coke' tattoo pays for itself.

Cigarettes are the preferred currency. One determined middle-aged man, gripping his lit cigarette through determined teeth, absent-mindedly soaped himself under the steaming shower. Someone else expertly flicked a customer's rump with a wet towel, also while smoking. A Buddha-weight businessman sat in the tub, talking on the phone, cigarette in his other hand. I don't generally smoke, even while swimming. Nor sing, even in the shower.

Men in bathhouses often break into musical without shame or concern. If there's a song on their mind, they do it. They just knock it out. I realize, now, that I could have bellowed a few power verses from something like Queen or Journey and no one would have said anything. But despite all the solo singing, acknowledgements between strangers were snorted – not spoken. I had previously considered this sort of greeting mostly the domain of pure pulp ("Malone grunted assent") but quickly got the hang of non-syllabic speech. I added a pathic nod as I grunted across to one man with a sprawling black dragon ascending his left arm and most of his shoulder.

He then wouldn't leave either of us alone. 'Dragon' caused my friend Jay particular anxiety with several vigorous handshakes, wagging his eyebrows for too long to be harmless. "What did that mean?" Jay asked after in a hush. "What does he want?"

"It's probably nothing. Just something to do with, you know … sex," I reassured him. "It's fine, we'll go through the next door."

Leaving the changing area, you troop right into the main hall and take it in: two giant, steaming baths, and more showers than you could ever need (five). Dragon leapt into one of the tubs, and beckoned us to join. We pointedly climbed into the other one. Snub over, a peaceful calm soon settled. A mantra began to repeat: this was a place to relax and *forget* the modern world, its deadlines and demands. Here, there was only the low murmur of voices in conversation, the playful splash of water – the occasional resounding 'thwack' from the massage tables. Jay and I exchanged contented nods. This was what we'd come for, a soak of old Beijing before it dried up like a dusty old crone.

Suddenly, the guy with a dragon on his back was on the move, clambering over the divide – the *divide* – and sinking into our bath. He kept his hands clasped nonchalantly behind his back, then began flicking water coquettishly on himself and at us. A coded signal? Local ritual? Haze the newcomers? He waded around, veered off, circled back, always smiling, nodding, splashing water, a pattern that continued until Jay finally broke the void and put it out there.

"Do you think he's gay? I think he thinks we like him now."

Dragon was yards away, oblivious to our commentary. Inches.

"Don't make eye contact. Pretend he's not there."

"Eye contact?" Jay's scowl couldn't contain the impending mirth. "His dick's about a foot from my face."

That was true, irrefutably so. But it was a bathhouse – he had the right of way. I gave Dragon a terse smile dovetailing into a slight frown (the English way of telling someone to fuck off, I presume you know it?), and saw that his cheeks had turned a bright scarlet. Just then he reached over, tapped Jay warmly on the shoulder, and launched himself out of the water, like a humpback whale. He didn't land like one: his heel slipped on a puddle, somersaulting him onto his buttocks and back. You winced to watch it, but he was back on his feet within seconds, giving the room a reassuring smile, like a true professional, before limping off with the same agonized grimace. As soon as he hit the changing-room door, though, the whole act collapsed. Brimming with tears, his eyes lurched between pain, jangled embarrassment and, finally, the irreversible frustration of enduring a plain old fuck-up.

"Aww," Jay conceded. "He's drunk."

Silently toasting Dragon's departure, we opted for the sauna. According to a warning sign outside, drinking "while steaming" is not something the Chinese staff recommend – along with being pregnant, childish or enduring any heat found within for longer than about ten minutes. Cocooned in the back of the Finnish-style commode, flipping the bird at all of these, was Hong Sheng. He was 56, athletically built – a master at practicing limber yogic splits on tile-floored baths – and garrulous. He began gabbing the moment we sat down, introducing himself as a "TCM master" who had been practicing certain techniques, passed down through the Hong family since the Tang Dynasty, for over four decades.

A self-proclaimed *qigong* master, Hong was. *Qigong* is the ancient practice of duping superstitious fat cats into handing over large sums of cash by performing cheap magic tricks. "I can wear the shortest shorts in winter and be completely comfortable," Hong cheerfully vouchsafed from his lotus position, streaming sweat as he ladled more water on the sizzling coals. "I can make water boil. I can make lights illuminate. Without electricity." Prove it, you swine, I panted internally: Turn this heat down.

"Throughout history, people have perceived us as either gods or fools – or worse, madmen," Hong lamented, presumably talking about *qigong* again. "Would you believe it if I told you I have actually spent some time in a mental hospital?" We would. If that wasn't the grimmest times of his life, it was up there – two months in a pitiless psychiatric ward run on medieval thinking, back in 2006. "I often thought about suicide," he muttered, punctuating the remark with a rip-roaring fart while pouring still more water on the screeching rocks. Along with his spiel, Hong had the scars to prove it and invited us to peer at the marks on his muscular, twisted frame "from the operations I did on myself."

The squat, silent fellow beside us had absorbed this whole conversation, all the while without stirring. But once our *qigong* master reluctantly left to his nude splits (performed on the wet divide of the baths), the stranger leaned over to make his own confession. "In Beijing dialect," he warned, "that's called bullshit."

It was surely time to leave this hot, drunken idyll and venture into the bone-freezing reality of a night in deepest December. And there were those donkey dumplings we had seen advertised nearby to look forward to. While we donned our winter ensemble (leg warmers, vest, heavy-duty sweater, hat, boots, scarf, muffler, ski goggles), Hong stopped by to bid an extended farewell, list a few more qualifications and offer a possibly free consultation. Despite the frostbite lurking outside, Hong was wearing only a loose cotton t-shirt and plain khaki shorts. Conceivably it was the ineffable blessing of a soak in Shuangxingtang that had warmed his soul. Possibly he should have been back in the psych ward. Then again, perhaps he really was an ancient mystic imbued with temperature-warping psychic abilities. Or maybe he just lived in that hotel next door.

Censor

Flash fiction

Alicia Lui

"JUST HOLD ME."

It started simply, with those words. Normally he wouldn't have taken a second look; they were harmless. As a censor at the largest social network company in China, all he had to do was scan thousands of messages daily to make sure "sensitive" messages didn't get out. But every now and then, to alleviate the boredom, he would read entire conversations: couples planning the weekend, company executives scouting apartments, teenage girls gossiping about cute boys – all manner of debates, jokes and puns. Most of them weren't that exciting, or original.

But they were more interesting than his own mundane and lonely life. No girlfriend, no family, no money, no passions … sometimes he wondered how he ever trudged through 25 years.

There was something different about *this* message. He couldn't quite explain it. *Just hold me.* There was nothing eye-catching about how it, nothing particularly revealing about the ID numbers. Nonetheless, he was riveted. He felt his throat tightening, so he swallowed. Why did the room suddenly feel so stuffy? His instincts told him to keep reading, to dig up past correspondences; he even felt an urge to reach out. But how? That was expressly forbidden, career suicidIt was almost midnight. Eight hours until his shift's end. He got up, told a colleague he needed some fresh air, and darted out before he could hear the reply. Up the elevator to the top floor, through a door to a stairwell and onto the roof. He stared down onto the streets. Emptiness. He imagined hundreds of people streaming out of their workplaces toward their cars, their bus stations, their homes.

In fact all he saw were the drab moons of streetlamps. He felt small and insignificant. A nobody. How many people did Beijing have? Twenty-one million, officials said, but he knew official statistics weren't to be trusted. There were more.

Were the people whose messages he read every day among those who had, hours before, walked the streets below? Was the girl also there? The one with the long black hair and fair white skin and pretty eyes and vanilla scent who'd written, "Just hold me". Was she another nobody like him, lost, pushed forward by those behind her, desperate for space to stop and breathe but enjoying none because the purpose of living is to keep moving? He leaned against the ledge and closed his eyes in the heat of the summer night.

He woke with a jolt. The sun was already above him.

"*Shit!*" he screamed. His voice reverberated. His phone said 7:40 am. He stood up and looked around. Emptiness still. The echo of his voice seemed to rouse him. He needed to be back at his seat for the end of his shift. His manager always walked in just before eight.

He woke his computer. The words "Just hold me" had long disappeared, replaced by messages that looked like hieroglyphics to his bleary eyes. Ten minutes. That's all he needed to wait out. His colleague had already left, maybe because there hadn't been much work. But was that possible? He scrolled and scrolled: the messages seemed endless.

"Time to go home, isn't it?"

That was the manager, right on time.

"Yeah."

And then he was outside, walking against the crowd in a magically crowded Zhongguancun subway station, a fish swimming upstream.

It was only on the train, his mind drifting between day and night dreams, that it occurred to him to wonder what messages he had let slip through in those absent hours. Maybe something important. Maybe something that would change the very sun rising this very moment above his world.

MADE IN CHINA
A quarter century in Chinese manufacturing

Laszlo Montgomery

CHINESE TRADE WITH the West has a history that reaches all the way back to the times of the Han Dynasty adventurer Zhang Qian in the second century BC. The allure of Chinese goods has always been exotic and unique. Silk, tea, lacquerware and other valuables ware sold along fabled trade routes to all points between Rome and Asia. The Silk Road, the Tea Horse Road, Marco Polo, Zheng He, Macao, the Canton System. For an old China hand like me, what isn't there to love about this rich history of trade with China?

But when I first started following the China story, back in the day, I had no idea that in my professional life I would become part of it myself.

My first job out of college was at a Hong Kong, starting in September 1989. I had graduated from college in the US with a History and Asian Studies degree, and sought out a China life that would allow me to use my language skills on the job. To find myself neck deep in this business was a dream come true. Based in Hong Kong, a typical mainland China trip was straight to the factories in Shenzhen or wherever else. I felt like Salieri, the Italian composer, when he finally got to Vienna in the 18th century. I had gone from reading about China to being a part of it. As it happened, I stayed in that crazy industry for the next twenty-five years.

Over the course of my career I worked for three Chinese manufacturers of consumer goods, two in Hong Kong and one in Ningbo. All three operations made stuff that lined the shelves of the big US retailers from coast to coast, and all three were real factories, not trading companies or middlemen. When buyers of "Made in China" merchandise did their product sourcing, they were looking for companies like mine. Behind us were hundreds of raw material suppliers and sub-contractors, but as far as our clients were concerned, the Chinese factory was the source. The buck stopped with us.

Wherever my work was, the job was essentially the same. As the sole Westerner in the company, I applied those home advantages to help them reel in more business. The company usually left the coddling of foreign clients to me, and a week rarely passed when I didn't have to placate an angry Western customer. Cozying up to Chinese officials in karaoke bars was also a regular gig, cooing to them to obtain maximum support for whatever it was we needed. Aside this innocent mischief there were others favors I had to take care of that weren't altogether legal and are better left unsaid.

The export manufacturing industry was the locomotive that pulled China's economy out of the mud in the 80s and 90s. It's said that five hundred million Chinese have been lifted out of poverty since the beginning of reform and opening up in 1978. Thank the factories and exporters like those I worked for. The changes China has gone through in the last thirty years are the ripple effect of millions upon millions of workers for these companies bringing their hard-earned yuan inland and spreading the wealth around.

When I look back on the early 90s, like an old codger who can't keep up with the times, I think that those were the good old days. No one can deny that China is still a land of great opportunity for fortune seekers – but in the business of getting sweatpants, writing pads, toys, household objects, hardware and all other manner of general merchandise to market, for a Chinese factory it just isn't what it used to be.

When the American consumer walks into Wal-Mart, Staples, Hobby Lobby, Big Lots or TJ Maxx, the volume of choice boggles the mind. Who hasn't walked into a Costco in the US for the first time, looked around and thought, what land of plenty is this? But for me, every merchandise display reminds me of a story or – more often – an incident. From the famous brands to the cheapo stuff, my guys made it all. That's great from a consumer standpoint, but it sucks for the Chinese factory. The supply chain from China to US distribution centers has now been tightened down to levels undreamed of thirty years ago.

Since Zhang Qian's days, the human relationship that solidified the buyer-seller relationship was an exporter's most prized and secret asset. With a dependable factory in place, anything was possible. If you were a mensch about doing business and the Chinese manufacturer liked you, they pull your company back from the brink of disaster. In the nineties, sourcing suppliers was still done the hard way. Unless you had an agent or an office in Hong Kong, you had to get on a plane, fly fourteen hours and go to a trade show in Hong Kong or Canton. The process was time consuming and laborious. But back then, with our mobile phones as big as a loaf of bread, we all marveled at the new technology.

Then came the Internet. Now both buyer and seller could find each other easily. In no time at all, the people I worked for became commoditized. The web had simplified the process of finding suppliers from two buying trips a year, in April and October, to a ten minutes search on Alibaba, Baidu or Google. Suddenly the outstanding merits of factories like mine became secondary to price. No matter how well a factory paid its workers, how consistent the quality was, how clean they were or how well they complied to safety regulations, if they didn't have a brand, all that took a back seat to offering the cheapest price.

All of a sudden, it was simple to slam that China price down to the bone marrow. All you had to do was find six to eight factories, ask them to quote your sample, and go with the lowest cost producer. If the factory you preferred wasn't the cheapest, you took the lowest price and waved it at your top choice, offering them a last chance. If the first choice factory didn't take the order, number two or three did. The prevailing thought on the Chinese factory end was that this money-losing order would open the door to future profitable opportunities. The Great Lie.

A few years ago, I took a step back and realized that the manufacturers making America's products faced an impossible future. The RMB was rising. There was a labor shortage. No matter how good the factories were, they were replaceable. Fungible. Once lionized, with vendor summits where awards were meted out to various categories of best factory, now they had become bile bears for big US retailers. Each of the companies I worked for employed between 2,500 and 5,000 people. That's a lot of paychecks, and the industry had become impersonal and mean. The world I had enjoyed for so long began to take on a bad smell.

As pressures mounted to slash costs and satisfy retailers' profit margins, quality was sacrificed and corners were cut. "Made in China" more than ever became synonymous with shoddy goods. But don't blame the Chinese for that. All the poorly made schlock that you put in your shopping basket at your local dollar store was signed off on by a buyer back home. If they said this piece of shit was good enough for the American consumer, the Chinese factory was happy to comply. Imagine how I felt sitting on the Chinese side of the table when some American retailer, for the sake of hitting a price point, gave the factory the thumbs up on a flimsier, cheaper material.

I followed my heart in 1989 and took the China path in life. I wasn't skilled at anything in particular, but I had learnt the language and let the waves carry me further in. It was a lucrative way to make a living, it took me to new places, and it allowed me to develop lasting friendships. Now I've amicably parted ways with the Ningbo-based manufacturer that was my last employer. For the time being, hanging out in Southern California and working on my China History Podcast takes up most of my days.

I recorded a podcast once on the life of Morris "two gun" Cohen, a Westerner who played a two-bit role in early Republican China as the bodyguard of Sun Yat-sen. Small and insignificant as he may have been, he still got to be there up close and watch history happen. I identify with Morris, in that I got to be part of the Chinese manufacturing glory days of the 80s and 90s. In the last years, I went to trade shows and saw row after row of booths for these once proud factories. They were kings once, all of them, punching out goods selling for less than $4.99 at retail, disparaged but bought all the same by the American consumer. Now they were fighting for their lives, and I wondered if they would be at that same booth next year or not.

Every China hand aspires to be a bridge between their country and the Middle Kingdom. In my twilight years I can look back fondly on my time as an American in the heyday of Made in China, playing my own bit part in China's economic miracle.

I'M NOT A COMMUNIST,
BUT I PLAY ONE ON TV

Life and times of a token white guy

Jonathan 'Cao Cao' Kos-Read

THE GUY WITH the world's biggest dick was on Howard Stern once.

Everybody was fascinated. Who wouldn't be? His dick was 14 inches long, as thick as a baby's arm. And everyone had questions: could he get it all the way in? Had he ever fucked a guy? Did erections make him light-headed? Pressing, important burning questions. But all the guy wanted to talk about was his novel – a long thing about intergenerational conflict and the struggle between morality and family and … or you know, something. Nobody was listening. They just wanted to know about his dick.

And honestly, I often feel the same way. I have a job that people think is interesting – both in an amusing way, but also as an odd sideways window into Chinese culture.

I play white guys in Chinese movies.

So I often get asked to write about it. But there is a problem. Before I came to China twenty years ago, I swore to myself I would never write that book. I used to browse the China section of bookstores – back when they existed. I wanted history, translations, novels. But the shelves were stuffed with "I went to China, did some random thing then wrote a stupid book about it". *River Town* is the most famous example – and one of the few not awful ones – but they're all basically the same: I went to China and studied kung fu and got changed, I went to China and taught English and learned about myself, I went to China and did something even more boring and learned/changed/ whatever. It's like a little sub-genre where people use China as a mirror for whatever neurosis they had coming in. It's not even like they're not genuine, they're just monotonous.

People could get away with it then because China was so unknown. No one had any idea what it was like and so people who went there were genuinely adventurous.

And I like to write about other things. I wrote an ancient China murder mystery novel for example! But nobody is interested. They just want to know what it's like to shoot a sex scene in Beijing, make zombie movies in Mongolia, and play kung fu cowboys.

And I get that. So it's been a long time since I lashed myself to the mast of my ship. The sirens have been twittering in my ear and the ropes are breaking, and finally I too have succumbed. So here are some excerpts from my take on:

"I went to China, did some random stuff and learned and whatever."

My bisexual orgy

I wondered if I could kiss a dude. I was on a Chinese web series. And it was during a two-year interval when Chinese directors had just started shooting narrative stuff for web distribution. For TV and film, there is a vast department of fussbudgets who squint at all content for broadcast. They're very thorough. And they gut Chinese entertainment – you can't shoot stuff people want to see. Cop shows are out because it would imply there was crime. Spy shows are out because no foreign spy could ever succeed. Comedy's out because you can't make poop and fart and sex and government jokes. That leaves "killing Japanese in WWII", which makes up about two-thirds of the filmed output here. And that gets dull quick.

But the Internet! It was an opportunity to redo the restrictions without going up against an entrenched government ministry! It was still fast and loose and people started to test boundaries! And Chinese patriots rose up on the Internet in a political firestorm to demand … just kidding.

They shot ass and boobs and stuff.

And that was how I found myself in the bisexual orgy. It was my final scene in what was a pretty good, daring show. I'm drowning my sorrows at losing the girl in a drunken fit of screwing and booze. On my left, millimeters from naked, are two eighteen-year-old Chinese models in nipple covers and g-strings. In front of me, also technically not naked is a Chinese dominatrix who occasionally moonlights making porn in Hong Kong, and and on my right, disconcertingly, are two dudes.

Now, I don't want to get into a "methinks he doth protest too much" monologue. I have no problem with gayness. I'm totally, 100% pro everything, zero hang-ups … or so I thought.

Because, when the camera started rolling, I had no problem feeling up the girls and the dominatrix but straight up, I felt super uncomfortable touching the dudes. I tried to rub their backs. I even went in for a kiss but pulled back at the last minute – all the time with my roving and hypocritical hands on the girls.

Now, what would have happened if the director had yelled cut and said "Jonathan, you're bisexual, you can't just touch the girls, you have to make out with a dude." What would I have done? I'm not actually sure.

Because the odd thing, the thing that most people back in America don't get is that gayness isn't a moral issue in China.

It's not evil to be gay. It's just *embarrassing*.

You don't get the nut job religious condemnation, but importantly you also don't get the moral validation for supporting a just cause when, for example, you play someone who is bisexual and REALLY GO FOR IT. You just get shrugs and snickers.

So I was writhing around on this bed in China in the 21st century. The cameras were rolling. I was trying to be a serious actor. But I chickened out.

I had my chance to kiss a dude for freedom. But I blew it.

Cheap foreign labor

The latest US election is hinging on whether Mexicans are criminals and rapists. Yes, say Republicans. No, say Mexicans. The issue, framed in the crappiest way possible, is "fucking stupid Mexicans can't get work in their shitty country so they come steal jobs from real Americans. Let's build a WALL to keep those assholes out!"

Now, it's easy to criticize that view at a distance. But then it happens to you.

This big Chinese movie called my agent and said, "We want Jonathan!" She asked for an outrageously high price and they said "Okay!", getting me in a pissed-off mood right away because it meant we could have asked for even more.

It's about Bruce Lee's kung fu teacher, Ip Man. It's representative of a big change in Chinese attitudes. Twenty years ago, Bruce was the hero because he MADE IT IN AMERICA. Now, though, his teacher has eclipsed him because he did the *honorable* thing and stayed in China thus preserving real honorable kung fu yada yada.

I signed the contract and they sent me the script. And immediately I got even more pissed off. There was ANOTHER

FOREIGNER in the movie and his part was OBVIOUSLY BIGGER than mine. So I texted the casting director, "Hey, cool script, who's this other foreigner?" No response. I waited a day and texted again, "Yeah, just wondering who's playing Frankie?"

No response. Total silent diss. I was irritated on the flight to Shanghai so I dissed them back by sulking in my hotel room before the shoot.

The next morning, I got into the van, got to the set, and immediately understood. There, on our location, in the middle of his entourage and looking a little bewildered, was Mike Tyson.

Honestly, I was intimidated. My teenage years were Iron Mike demolishing people in ten seconds. I walked over.

"Hi, I'm Jonathan. We're in the scene together."

He lisped out, "Hi, I'm Mike," in that startling voice he has.

"Yeah, I know who you are."

He shook my hand. I'd never been that close to so much physical power. It was overwhelming. Like shaking hands with Grendel.

And so the question arises: what was Mike Tyson doing in a Chinese movie?

American stars have been trickling into Chinese movies starting about five years ago. The producers hire them because they want the cachet. But can't afford the big stars. So they mostly get guys on the decline and second rankers. Those guys come partly because they need work and money, but more really to rejuvenate their careers. Because to be a leading actor in Hollywood now *you need Asian Box Office*. So just this year, guys like John Cusack, Adrian Brody and Nick Cage all shot here. Definitely stars, but they don't shine like they used to. This is a path back. And they come with a massive pay cut.

Cheap foreign labor stealing jobs.

And the result of this was that I spent three days hanging out with Mike Tyson. And I mean really hanging out. When you're acting, you're in a little bubble with your co-actor. Chaos swirls around you but you just sit and talk quietly. Mike Tyson, to my immense surprise, is, like, *the fucking nicest guy*. To give you a sense of it we:

1) Talked pre-schools.
We have daughters the same age. With Iron Mike, I compared Montessori methods, and talked about letting kids find their own way, blah blah. Concerned over-anxious parent stuff.

2) Talked philosophy.
"How come you didn't become a trainer after boxing?"
"Not my thing."
"Yeah, the best coaches were mediocre players. They had to be smart because they didn't have that magic."
"Nah, there's something more important. A lot of coaches failed and they're living their dreams through you.

3) Talked deep stuff.
"I watch a lot of industry girls hit thirty and get spit out and have to learn how to build a new life. That seems to be kinda, ahhmm, like you..."
"Yeah, that's me. Always startin' over."
"What are you doing now?"
"I like the acting."
"Really?"
"Yeah man."
"Why?"
"Cuz when I'm actin I don't have to be me."

That was SO not what I expected, like, a smart, thoughtful,

insightful guy. I really liked him, in the same way any Republican would probably like any INDIVIDUAL Mexican he met. And that's the rub. It's not his fault he's here. It's smart. It's what he *should be doing*. I know I can't fight it. I just have to work harder. And in the long run its good for my industry; a rising tide floats all boats. But my first reaction when these guys come over and take parts that I used to have a shot at is *always* that Donald Trump-style visceral gut paranoia.

It is what it is.

China basically sucked for the last hundred and fifty years. But now it's stepping back up into the position it has held for most of human history. And with that shift, the first real scattering of people is fluttering over in this direction. They're dropping into China because this is where the money and the excitement and the opportunities are. And more come every day.

Maybe China should build a wall too, or, ermm ... another one.

I want her to be fat

I have to admit, right up front, that I didn't write most of this last part. It was written instead by some random Chinese guy.

Below I have translated the best bits of an article entitled "Showbiz's Biggest Foreigner and How He Was Molded By His Young Wife Into a Chinese Style Husband". It's from a Chinese magazine and it's about how I met and fell in love with my wife. I got it as an email attachment with a cute note that said, in Chinese: "Hey, we were just like *super* inspired by your story so we wanted to profile you in our magazine but, you know, our deadline was like, *super* soon so, like, we didn't have time to interview you."

It's so awesome I'm worried you'll think I added shit to make it funnier but I didn't. What you read below is really a verbatim translation. So kind of like Long Duc Dong in *Sixteen Candles* and Han in *Two Broke Girls*, this is how Chinese see Americans.

Cao Cao's Love Story

Endless, repetitive, monotonous work was drowning Jonathan in feelings of suffering and helplessness. He was desperate to find a girlfriend. He begged all his friends for introductions to Chinese girls. But he found fault in each one. None were good enough.

He fell into depression. His friends criticized him for being too picky. Finally when he pleaded yet again, his friend shot back exasperated, "Well what kind of girl do you want?!"

Jonathan said, "I don't want a naïve girl. And I don't want one who follows orders. I want her to be fat. "

"Ha ha," his friend said, "I actually know such a girl. Her name is Li Zhiyin. She is a junior at the Capital University of Finance. She is fat."

In short order, Jonathan and Li Zhiyin were shepherded to a Sanlitun coffee shop by this friend. Jonathan had made a special and extraordinary effort of personal grooming. And when he saw Li Zhiyin for the first time he saluted her in the Chinese, double-raised-fist style. He said in ancient Chinese, "I am Cao Cao, please forgive any obstreperousness or importune mistakes made by my humble self."

Here it drags for a bit. But then disaster strikes:

Li Zhiyin began to feel this American young man was serious and honest so her initial wariness was dropping away.

But then Jonathan told her a story, "When I first told my friends I was coming to China they told me I must bring toilet paper." Jonathan laughed heartily at the ironic humor inherent in this. "According to these American friends of mine, China –"

But before Jonathan could finish, Li Zhiyin's face turned a dark shade of angry red. She said, "It is true! Our Mother Country is not rich! But we will Self Empower, Self Strengthen and Self Stand Up!" Then Li Zhiyin stood erect, and proudly and angrily stomped out of the coffee shop. Jonathan desperately followed her saying, "I did not mean that those friends are correct! I was telling you a funny story!" Li Zhiyin threw off Jonathan's hand and said with ire, "If I made a joke about America, what would you do?!" Then she gave Jonathan a dangerous, strong and proud glare. Jonathan was struck speechless and frozen by this.

"This," Jonathan thought, "is a proud girl. I must change the angle of my thinking to be with her."

We hook up, and everything is great for a while, but then, again (if only my real life were so dramatic) disaster.

Unskilled in business, Jonathan was wracked with terrible difficulties maintaining his company for [those] three years. In the end, all of the money he had earned with his heart's blood was lost.

After his bankruptcy, he was left only with a heart depressed and a mind frozen. In the beginning he had dreamed of giving Li Zhiyin a good life! Who would have thought that now he couldn't even support himself?! Controlling the agony in his heart, he wrote a breakup letter to Li Zhiyin. It said that his business venture had failed.

"I even tried to return to being an English teacher but no one would have me!"

He remonstrated with Li Zhiyin to take care of herself,

because he must go away - like an ancient, itinerant traveler, to float, to drift alone in the emptiness between the earth and the sky.

When Li Zhiyin saw his letter her heart was stabbed with pain. She rushed to his home. But his apartment was already empty! She called him. His cellphone had been turned off! Li Zhiyin wildly dialed all of Jonathan's friends, every one. Finally she learned the truth – he had left on a quest to discover the true meaning and location of the Three Kingdoms Romance [from which he had taken his Chinese name].

Such an enormous country China! Li Zhiyin decided she would first go to Weiwang, the ancient and original Cao Cao's ancestral home in Anhui, Haozhou. In Haozhou she bitterly and with great difficulty searched for three days. Finally deep inside Cao Cao's famous tunnel for transferring soldiers, she found a cowering Jonathan, whole body covered in dirt, stained, face fatigued, depressed and defeated.

She yelled, "Jonathan!"

She lifted her bag and struck him again and again and again. Jonathan knelt on the ground cradling his head in his hands and accepted the blows.

Finally with no strength left Li Zhiyin ceased her blows. She yelled, "who told you to leave?! What will I do without you?!"

Jonathan, his eyes red-rimmed, said, "I am bankrupt! My own life, I can't even support-"

"Tea!"

"Tea," Li Zhiyin said again. "It must be steeped in the hottest water to draw out the deepest flavor! People are the same. Only by facing the hot forge of disastrous difficulties can a man become strong and oriented to succeed. I Believe you can succeed!" said Li Zhiyin as she held his hand tightly.

"But if I can never succeed?" said Jonathan, his face pale

and shadowed.

"Silly melon! In that case we will simply live a quiet life. The world is so big, how many people in the world can succeed?! If we can live with open happy hearts, this is enough! Return with me!"

Needless to say, I did. And our happy ending took place in the warm twinkling glow of blinking lights:

The very day that the interior decoration was finally completed, Jonathan brought his wife Li Zhiyin to take possession of their new home. The very moment they stepped through the door, the very first sight that passed Li Zhiyin's eyelids was a large square pool in their living room. Within the water were seven brightly lit electric water lilies of seven different blinking colors.

"This is our 'Seven Color Lily Pool'. In the future our life will be like these lilies – many styles, many poses, many colors," said Jonathan as he looked at Li Zhiyin and tenderly smiled.

Li Zhiyin threw her arms around his neck in a deep and strong embrace.

There is much more awesomeness to this story, but the tyranny of the word count restricts me. So alas, I must chuckle alone.

And so, have we been enlightened? Have ave we gained some deeper insight into the creative process, the mind of the artist?

Some say that the Chinese are not creative, that they simply copy the creativity of others. Psshhaww! Here I am the counterfeiter, stealing the work of another for my own dirty gain. The quiet tinkerer who created this piece was the true artist.

He googled the world, found truth and created beauty.

In summation

I've lived in China for almost twenty years, my entire adult life. For seventeen of those years I've made films. And so those questions: What did I learn? How was I changed?

There is a wonderful moment in the opening paragraphs of Conrad's *Heart of Darkness* when the narrator describes stories. Those of an average sailor, he says, "have a direct simplicity, the whole meaning of which lies within the shell of a cracked nut."

But Marlow, the man who travels to a distant and strange place, is different:

> *To him the meaning of an episode was not inside like a kernel but outside, enveloping the tale which brought it out only as a glow brings out a haze …*

OLD CHOKEY CHRISTMAS

Festive doggerel

—————

Kaiser Kuo

In winter all's still, and the sun's scanty rays
Filter downward in pewter and silvery grays.
I find myself strolling down memory *hutong*
To Beijing in winters when life was more *putong*.

Glazed roof-tiles girded in glistening icicles,
Sonorous bells on still-plentiful bicycles,
Cabbages, coal smoke, and good *shuanyangrou,*
And sidewalks all covered in soot-blackened snow.

The winters seemed colder, and Houhai would freeze,
While the snow would collect on the boughs of the trees.
It's rare now to see cabbage stacked on the stoop
Which by springtime would rot to gelatinous goop.

The tempting aromas of sugar-fried *lizi,*
And yams baked in oil drums wafts to your *bizi.*
Or sweet crunchy skewers of red candied haw
Which are no longer sold come the early spring thaw.

No Christmastime feasts back then, nothing so grand.
We McGyvered it up with what scraps were at hand.

Instead of the turkey and after-eight brandy,
We guzzled Yanjing and ate White Rabbit candy.

It may be the earth has been globally warmed.
It may be my memory by time's been transformed.
But winter these days doesn't feel so romantic,
As the pace of life toggles 'twixt hectic and frantic.

Modernity offers its own winter charms
(Though I'm not sure it helps more than it harms).
Both April Gourmet, and of course Jenny Lou's,
Offer comfort-food cures for our grim winter blues.

And with broadband these days, the chill might not trouble you
Even considering the damned GFW.
Though Internet blockages make us quite bitter,
We still manage access to Facebook and Twitter.

The Web offers so many ways to enjoy
All those holiday classics I loved as a boy.
I sit by my space heater, warm in my *qiuku*,
And stream "It's a Wonderful Life" off of Youku.

We send SMS to spread holiday cheer,
In Nativity missives at least half-sincere
And Hanukkah greetings as well if you choose
(Since half of the gringos in Beijing are Jews).

The net has made giving of gifts all too easy
From *zhengban* to *shanzhai*, from tawdry to cheesy.
And what could beat Taobao for buying your presents,
To have them delivered by tricycling peasants?

The traffic gets bad, but it's bad in each season,
To get me to cross town, you'll need a good reason.
I normally don't mind the subway at all,
At least in the spring, or the summer, or fall.

But with everyone wearing a fluffy down jacket,
Each subway car needs extra staff just to pack it.
They shove you inside just as hard as they can,
Like they do for the rush hour trains in Japan.

Come winter, the nightlife does not drop a beat.
The revelers give off enough body heat.
The bars are decked out in the Christmas decor,
meaning lights they've left up since the season before.

Hot Toddies and mulled wine and egg nog with rum
(Though prices, I fear, are a princely-ass sum),
With globalisation, wherever you roam,
The holidays won't be too different from home.

But I wonder if that's what it should be about.
With each passing winter comes reason to doubt.
So for Christmas this year I'm inclined more than not
To dine with the family on mutton hot pot.

As for wintertime goodies completely indigenous,
Is goose all that better than fine roasted pigeon is?
An Old Chokey Christmas – now what could be finer
Than spending the holidays right here in China?

It's the small things, they say, that make life worth living.
Intentions, not price tags, make gifts worth the giving.

Those home comforts can't match the fresh-candied haws
Or the chestnuts or yams – suck on *that*, Santa Claus!

Family Footsteps

Finding home for Spring Festival

Peta Zhimin Rush

It's Chinese New Year, which means red paper couplets, decorations and lanterns are being hung up, and firecrackers are going off every evening like gunfire. For those who live away from their ancestral home, it also means taking part in the largest annual human migration in history to return home for the holidays, often involving a 30 hour crowded train journey halfway across the country.

I would do the same, if I knew where mine was.

One of the reasons why I came to China was to discover my own ancestral home. I am a "mixed blood" child, a *hunxue'er*, and grew up in Singapore before moving to England when I was seven. My father is English but my mother was ethnically Chinese. Along with many others from the landed classes, her parents fled China during the first civil war of 1927-1937, when the Nationalists and Communists were vying for control of the country. Some of my family went to Indonesia and Hong Kong, but my maternal grandparents settled in Singapore.

They raised their four children in a humble *kampong*, a settlement of very basic village housing. In the early 70s, when my mother was growing up, Singapore wasn't the booming financial city it is today. But even by the standards of the time, my mother's upbringing was a tough one. She once told me of her acute embarrassment when, at her primary school's annual medical check, she had to wait in line in her home-made cloth underwear while her classmates wore shop-bought knickers with proper elastic.

At home, they mostly ate rice bulked out with pickled vegetables. My mother said she was able to eat four bowls of rice for dinner, despite remaining beanpole thin. The fruit and vegetables were usually the half-rotten kind that are sold at discount at markets. As a child, my mother only once ate "perfect" fruit – when she was ill, a family friend brought her a whole bunch of grapes. I remember getting an earful as a child when I tried to throw away a half-rotten apple. Then there was the chicken they kept in the bathroom, feeding with scraps from the family table before slaughtering it for the Chinese new year reunion dinner. Each year there was a new "toilet chicken", and as a child my mother was torn between sympathy for the family pet and excitement about eating it.

I grew up with the stories my mother told me of my Chinese ancestral history. My grandfather was from a wealthy landowning family in Guangdong province, one of seven children. Among his sisters one died as a child, after accidentally being given rat poison instead of cough medicine, both of which were kept on the same shelf in the kitchen. My grandmother's elder sister, meanwhile, had her feet bound—an extremely painful ritual where the bones of a young girl's feet are broken, then bound tightly with bandages so they can't heal properly, leaving the desired "lotus feet".

When my great aunt's feet were bound, according to my mother, she screamed so much that after a few months her mother finally relented and took the bandages off. Her broken feet were allowed to grow, but she had difficulty walking for the rest of her life. I remember visiting her many times as a child in Singapore, bringing her crates of duty free cigarettes from England and enduring the customary cheek pinch bestowed by Chinese elders on every child. Despite smoking 60 cigarettes a day, she long outlived my grandmother, who died when I was one month old.

My grandparents had married in their teens, but my grandfather was a favored and spoilt son, and his newfound independence in Singapore allowed him to indulge his gambling habit. He lost most of their savings early on in the marriage, and his family soon stopped sending him money. He found work as a ship's carpenter, and started to live a more honest life. My family still has a beautiful wooden chest which was made by him. He eventually died of throat cancer, after inhaling fumes from the tar with which he used to coat the decks of the ships, to help them withstand seawater.

When my grandfather was away at sea, my grandmother spent all her time playing mahjong. My mother told me she would often come home from school to a dark house, unable to turn on the lights as she was too small to reach the switch. When she went to find her mother at the mahjong parlor, if the game was going well she would get a dollar with which to buy herself noodles for dinner. If her mother was doing badly, she would get a smack instead and no money for food. She often went to bed hungry, or turned to her oldest brother, who had already left school to work. The pocket money he gave her was the main reason she could complete her schooling.

My mother died while I was still at school, and whole chapters of her and my grandparents' story are missing. Back then I didn't have much interest in my Chinese heritage — I was more concerned with being as Western as possible. Now that she is gone, and my connection with China is fading, it's more important to me than ever to find a link with that side of my family. As *hunxue'er* go I look pretty Western, which has never bothered me in the past. Now that I'm living in China, studying Chinese and teaching English in Chengdu, I go out of my way to convince colleagues and friends that I really am half Chinese. I suspect many of them still don't believe me. If you're half Chinese, they ask me, why can't you speak Mandarin?

My older brother and I used to talk about the confusion we feel when someone asks where we are from. As mixed-race migrants, the options for our response are greater than for most. Do they want to know where we lived for most of our childhood, or why we look "different"? Are they asking where we were born, or where we live now? Or are they really asking where our parents are from? I thought that if I returned to my ancestral home in Guangdong, the village where my grandparents were born, I could finally find somewhere I properly belong. By retracing the steps my family took all those years ago, maybe I would gain a better understanding of where I come from and who I am.

When I first came to China in 2013, finding my ancestral home seemed an impossible task. I didn't know the name of the village, and all I knew about the location was that it was somewhere near a river, in an area where Seiyap, a regional dialect of Cantonese, was spoken – which narrowed it down to the greater Taishan area, with a population of roughly four million. I didn't even know the character for my own grandfather's surname. At home, my grandparents were always *gonggong* and *pohpoh*. Because Singapore was under British rule when they immigrated, their surname was recorded as Kong, a phonetic spelling of the Cantonese pronunciation, and could be any of a number of characters.

A year and a half into my time in Chengdu I took a trip back to Singapore, and for the first time in 27 years I was able to communicate in the same language as my mother's elder sister, my *yima*, who only speaks Chinese. She was able to add a few more pieces to the jigsaw of my family's history. I now know my grandfather's name was Kuang Xiuzhuo. And thanks to the sleuthing of a friend in Chengdu who used to be a policeman, I know that he came from a small village called Shuikou, next to a river to the southwest of Guangzhou. Before I go back to England, I'll be making the trip to Shuikou to ask if anything remains of my old family home, or if anyone there remembers Kuang Xiuzhuo, who set out with his young wife on a boat to leave China all those years ago. But between civil war, the Mao era and China's current pace of development, I doubt anything will remain of his house. As landowners, his family's property would likely have been ransacked by the Red Guards, with anything of worth looted or destroyed. Even if it's still standing, all I have is a decaying photograph of the main room to identify it by.

Nor am I so sure any more if finding that house will give me any deeper knowledge about myself and my background. In her book *Factory Girls* the journalist Leslie Chang describes visiting her ancestral home for the first time. "A family is not a piece of land," she writes. "It is the people who belong to it, and it is the events that shape their lives." In the same way, my own search for home has been more about threading together the narrative of my family's past. The physical place itself isn't where my Chinese heritage can be found. It exists in the stories that were passed down from my grandparents to my mother to me. It was those stories that prompted me to return to China, and to reconnect with a side of me I thought I had lost forever.

That way, the story won't end with me.

Short Nails, White Socks

Fiction

Magdalena Navarro

Auntie Han took two steps back and looked at me as if straightening a crooked painting.

"Are you wearing the new socks?"

She stepped forward to flatten my hair to the sides of my head.

"Yes." Plain white, no patterns. I had changed into them at the train station that morning.

"Hmm. Show me your hands."

I obeyed, my eyes fixed on her mouth. Two of her front teeth were missing, but that did not make her look endearing. She was getting them fixed now that she had saved a bit of money. Besides, her mother-in-law's funeral had given her an excuse to go back home for a while. I was her replacement.

"Good." She dropped my hands. "Keep your nails clean and short. That's how they like it."

I nodded and fumbled with the zipper of my jacket while she registered me with the guards at the gate.

"All you have to do is keep everything tidy," Auntie Han said as we walked past rows of large red brick houses. "The Philips don't have children and they're never home for lunch, so it's not hard. Just make the bed, do the laundry and water the plants. Oh, and walk the dogs. They're very nice. You can talk to them in Chinese, they're from a shelter in Beijing. Now when we go inside let me do the talking. They already know about you. And shake their hands the way I told you, looking into their eyes."

When we arrived, I did as I was told. I was slightly disappointed because I had hoped for a more foreign color, but their eyes were just brown, like mine. That wouldn't make for such an interesting story back home. But the Philips seemed kind and repeated my name several times, tilting their heads.

"Am I saying that correctly?" Mrs. Philips asked each time. She wasn't, but I smiled anyway.

As Auntie Han kept talking, I glanced down at my gleaming new white socks. They seemed to be sinking into the grey carpet that covered the whole room like soft, furry concrete. The room's few furnishings were oddly shaped; the chairs strangely low, as if they had stopped growing at a certain point. In a corner by the big window, three long and narrow black vases pointed their empty mouths to a ceiling as bare as the walls. Why was a room this large so empty? I thought diplomats were supposed to be rich. Had they just moved in?

"Li Ying, would you like to meet the dogs?" my aunt asked, so sweetly I knew she was performing. I smiled and Mr. Phillips went to let them out of the guest room.

Buttons was white and tiny and had to be kept on a leash at all times because she had a problem with authority. Zipper was beer-colored and extremely obedient. I was supposed to wipe their paws whenever we came back from a walk. If any food fell on the floor, I was to throw it away immediately, even if it had only been a few seconds.

"Just remember to wash the whites separately," Auntie Han repeated for the hundredth time right before she left. "You'll be all right."

The first few days were lonely. I paced around the apartment feeling my stomach churn. I hadn't noticed how eerily quiet it was until then. Back home, silence was textured with creaking floorboards and whistling kettles; it was thin and flimsy and never prevailed over the baby next door or the landlord's TV. But this was a deeper silence, thick and absolute, a quilted void upon which life left no trace. I didn't dare to turn on the TV and couldn't figure out their glossy music system either, so I started talking to the dogs instead.

It was Buttons and Zipper that led me to the Stone Circle for the first time. Auntie Han had told me there were around thirty women working for families in the compound, but only nine showed up at the garden every morning at ten o'clock. On the grass, now yellow and parched, stone benches and tables were arranged in a circle around a metal grill, covered by a canvas. Some of the aunties arrived with dogs, some with children, but all of them wore similar puffy down jackets and big Korean perms.

Like me, most were from the Northeast, so we quickly fell into dialect. They all knew who I was and told me how good my aunt would look when her teeth were fixed. We were talking about how cold March had been when someone hushed us.

"Shh! Here she comes now!"

A woman in a mauve fleece jacket and carrying a green plastic thermos approached behind a little girl with light brown hair and a puffy purple jacket. They stopped directly in front of me and the woman spoke.

"You must be Xiao Han's niece! When did you arrive in Beijing?"

"A few days ago, on the train from Harbin," I said.

She had a pleasant face, flat and smooth, like a pebble in a riverbed. Her hair was tightly coiled into a bun on top of her head. Two small hoops of gold had torn their way through her earlobes over the years, pulling them down, making her look like a Buddha. On her collar there was a smudgy star-shaped sticker. Her nails were short and clean.

I must have looked confused because another of the aunties spoke up.

"Li Ying, this is Auntie Yu," she said, gesturing to the woman. "We all look up to her here. She is a friend of the ambassador's wife!"

Auntie Yu let out a single dry laugh and shook her hand dismissively.

"Please, Xiao Ma, that was ages ago! That was the old ambassador's wife. I don't know the new one all that well," she sighed. "Besides, I'm getting too old. Soon they'll have no use for me here, with so many young faces ..." she looked at me and smiled again. "You must call me Auntie."

"Thank you, Auntie." It was impossible not to smile back at a face like that.

"Good, good." She pointed her green thermos at one of the red brick houses behind us. "Well, we must get going. Today is Sara's birthday and they'll want us inside." She looked down at the little girl and gave her a squeeze on the shoulder. "Sara, tell the aunties how old are you today."

Sara was busy trying to reattach a race car sticker to her jacket. She looked at us shyly and then tugged on Auntie Yu's jacket to whisper in her ear.

"No, that was last year," she whispered back. "How old are you this year?"

Sara extended five hesitant fingers and smiled when the women burst into a choir of praise.

"Well, there you go! Say bye-bye now. Bye bye, Xiao Ma! Bye-bye, Xiao Li!" they waved.

We all waved goodbye back. The moment Auntie Yu disappeared, Auntie Ma hissed slowly, poisoning every syllable, "Stupid conceited cow."

I looked at her, surprised. Her face had turned a virulent red.

"One year! She's just one year older than me and she calls me Xiao Ma! Can you believe it?" The women shook their heads in sympathy. "Like I'm some twelve-year-old schoolgirl or something!"

"Everyone hates Auntie Yu," she went on, "even the dogs. The airs she puts on! She's only here because her good-for-nothing of a husband used to drive around the ambassador, a million years ago. Someone made her a resumé in English and that's how she gets the best jobs."

"The foreigners don't know anything," another auntie put in. "They're completely clueless. Someone makes a recommendation and they all follow blindly, as if she was the only one with experience. You know what Auntie Yu says on her resumé?" She didn't wait for me to shake my head. "She claims that she has raised seventeen foreign children and taught them all Chinese! Isn't that rich! Teach! Teach what? She can barely write, the moron!"

"It's not just the baby-sitting," Auntie Ma said. "Auntie Yu also convinced the foreigners to give her all their recyclables so she can cash them in! She snuck behind our backs and went door to door telling them to keep the bottles for her!"

"Can't you just tell your families to give them to you instead?" I asked.

"That old lizard could make sure I don't work again! She knows people. The diplomats come and go, but we stay here." She stared at the space where Auntie Yu had been before. "I'm not going back home."

The aunties of the Stone Circle loved speculating about how unhappy their employers were. They saw depression in a few empty bottles in the trash, anxiety in tags still dangling from dresses purchased months ago. The aunties didn't gloat about it, but there was a glimmer of pleasure when the talked about the dark side of wealth.

The dogs couldn't be happier, though. They were a source of joy for the aunties, who discussed them at length, comparing them and projecting on them traits of their own personalities. Loki was easy-going like Auntie Xi. Rufus hated lamb, just like Auntie Wang. Many of them had been taking care of the dogs for so long, they felt closer to the animals than their owners. They sighed and said things like: "I just don't know what will happen to Copper when they leave." Without the aunties, the dogs would be just as unhappy as their owners.

But no topic filled the silence quite like Auntie Yu. Though she never physically joined us at the Stone Circle, everyone always seemed to know where she was and what she was doing. I saw Auntie Yu teaching the gardener how to plant trees. Auntie Yu told me she doesn't use any beauty products, it's just her northeastern blood. Auntie Yu recommends using a slice of lemon to whiten your teeth.

Since I was new, I had very little gossip to contribute, but they all became excited when I said I sometimes ran into Auntie Yu on my way out of the compound.

"You must talk to her!" they chirped. "You're new, she'll want to talk to you!"

"And you must tell us what she says," added Auntie Ma.

And so I lingered near the compound's poorly lit passage after work the following day, hoping to hear the telltale clinking of her recyclables. She was unusually late and it was very cold. I had already turned to leave when I heard her footsteps emerge under the orange glow of the streetlamp.

"Li Ying!" a voice called. I was surprised to see the little girl walking by Auntie Yu's side, her face puffy and red, as if she had been crying. "You got off late today."

"Uh, yes. So much to do," I mumbled.

If she noticed my nervousness, she didn't mention it.

"Sara dropped her stickers," she said. "We need to find them so she can go to bed. Would you help us?"

I really had no reason not to, although I felt guilty thinking of the women at the Stone Circle. I pulled my jacket tighter and followed them into the dimly lit garden. Sara Hawthorne led the way, tugging at Auntie Yu's arm until she finally let her run. I took my cellphone out and used the light from the screen to look for the stickers.

"I remember when your aunt started working here, long ago," said Auntie Yu as we walked the gardens. She was looking at the ground too, although she had no light. "She wasn't even married yet. The train broke down before it reached the city and she had to walk for hours to make it here on time for her interview. She's a proud woman, your aunt. She didn't want to ruin her good shoes, so she walked all the way here in her socks." Auntie Yu laughed softly. "I had to lend her mine before she changed, you know?"

I didn't know what to say. Shame pressed hotly against the skin of my face. But before I could force myself to speak, Sara squealed with delight and ran over to us waving the stickers in her hand. She rewarded Auntie Yu with two of them and she gave me one as well, insisting that I stick it to my collar immediately. It was a small red race car with a yellow stripe and a big smile.

The next day, the women at the Stone Circle asked me if I had run into Auntie Yu the night before. I could feel Auntie Ma's eyes on the sticker on my collar.

"It was too cold to wait," I said, sinking my hands in my pockets. "I went straight home".

It was almost a week until I ran into Auntie Yu again. She was alone this time, and asked me if I wanted to ride the bus with her, since we were going in the same direction. If I had known it would be the last time we would see each other, I wouldn't have bothered with all the pleasantries about how cold the spring was or complained about how difficult it was to find a seat on the morning bus. We would have talked. I would have spent more time looking at her face, trying to understand why anyone would hate it. But I thought all that could wait.

It was Zipper who let me know something was wrong the following day. Buttons was so loud that her barking wasn't news, but I had never seen Zipper so agitated. She was pacing anxiously by the window, whining dolefully. I turned off the vacuum cleaner and called them over, but neither acknowledged me, which was strange. I took them outside, and as soon as we reached the garden I realized we weren't the only ones. There were six or seven foreigners in suits walking around and talking rapidly. The guards peered in from their posts. All the women from the Stone Circle were already there, standing under the pale sun. Two were sobbing.

"What happened?" I asked.

They all started talking at the same time, unable to listen to each other. Sara Hawthorne was dead. She had gone to sleep and not woken up again, no matter how many times her mother had shaken her and called her name. Someone had seen an ambulance rush in around six that morning with the flashing lights on, but soon after they had been turned off because there was no rush, not anymore. People were going in and out of the Hawthornes'. All over the compound the dogs had started barking and there was no quieting them, because they seemed to know. They knew before anyone else.

"And Auntie Yu?" I asked.

"The guards said she left with the ambulance," someone said. "She was only wearing one shoe."

I stood dumbly next to the group, unable to stop thinking of Auntie Yu and the shoe she wasn't wearing.

"A terrible tragedy," said Auntie Ma finally. Her mouth was a thin line.

"Terribly unlucky," sighed someone.

"Who, Auntie Yu?" Auntie Ma said. "No, she's not unlucky. Think about it, she's had a long career. She's lucky that it happened now that she's old; she already made her money. Now she'll finally be able to retire." She looked at me and smiled faintly. "And make way for new arrivals."

I stared at Auntie Ma in silence. I didn't know where to start. My eyes felt white hot, almost incandescent in their sockets. I held her gaze until I burned the smile off her face, until everybody quieted down and watched the two of us. Their eyes never left me, not even when I turned around and walked away. Not even when I left the compound.

Awkward Lavender

Framed in a wedding photo

Jesse Field

I WAS TOLD we would just be "looking at the flowers" – *kan hua'r* – on Saturday afternoon, in a lavender field in Huairou, north of Beijing. It was only my second year in China, but I had already lost my sense of surprised anticipation. I was ready to be jaded. We drove up in a sedan with my boyfriend at the time, Yuan Kuo, and two of his friends, Li Ning and Yang Yang, a boy and a girl silly in love with each other.

The other couple seemed nice but unremarkable, so I kept to myself. I didn't attempt to make conversation, though I followed theirs well enough and answered cheerfully any questions they asked. Yuan Kuo, meanwhile, combined backseat driving ("Oh, let's drive faster! You can pass there! Go on through!") and plain whininess ("Why do you have coca cola bottles in the back seat? The right hand side is getting too much sun!").

"Here, hand me your make-up and the swab," he said to Yang Yang at one point.

"Uhm, why?" she asked.

"I'm looking too dark. I need to lay down lightening foundation."

"Are you a boy or a girl?"

"Whatever you want me to be, babe."

This repartee annoyed and amused us by turns, but only

brought us closer together.

When we arrived at the lavender field, Yuan Kuo griped, full of the disappointment I felt but held in. It was only a couple of acres, and quite pretty in its way, but already a hundred or so people were mulling around the grounds. All of them were in bright white wedding costumes and fully made-up, trailed by professional photographers who cooed at them in the soft, indulgent imperatives of their profession. "Ok, ok, yessss. Now, pretty lady, get a little closer to your beau, right. Ah! Good shot! Now crouch down lower. Tilt your face towards me. No, too far! Back the other way! Tilt again! Back! Yesssss, there!"

There was one of these groups every few yards, and the field was scattered with photographic props – a fake white piano, a platform set up like a bridal bed with swishy sections of silk, a set of big white English letters on metal frames: LOVE, like the HOLLYWOOD sign in LA. I felt awkward trailing the young couple, who had obviously come here on a very serious pre-engagement date. Yang Yang had made wreaths of flowers and matching felt shoes in the shape of cute dogs for her and her man. Li Ning had brought a Canon SLR, and they took pictures in the field for the next two hours.

I tried to make the best of it by wandering off on my own. I watched the scattered lovers from a distance, and found a small farmhouse at the north end of the property. Outside was a garden, where red peppers dried in the sun, enormous winter melons hung off the vine, and a small coop of chickens clucked quietly. Turning my head back towards the lavender field, I realized that this was all a bee-keeping operation. The bees were the tourists. At some 20 or 30 yuan per car, they were a honey-sweet cash crop for the farm.

After some time I heard the unique sound of the name "Jesse" as pronounced by Yuan Kuo. It reminds me of the way my Grandma used to say it in her Gulf-coast Mississippi accent, pushing the middle "e" towards a long "a." But Grandma always put the word at the end of sentences: "My favorite grandson has always been my little Jesse." Yuan Kuo used it as a call to attention.

"Jaysee! Jaysseee! What are you doing? Come on!"

"Oh hi," I replied. "I was just ... thinking."

He frowned, hurt. He knew perfectly well that I had grown cooler towards him, that I was mulling over my situation, and likely to leave him any day.

"I was afraid you'd be bored, so I came over here to take pictures with you. Get your camera out."

"I was fine, really," I snapped. Yuan Kuo's Audrey-Hepburn pushiness, once so alluring, now got on my nerves. "It's taking pictures that bores me."

That came off too harsh. I didn't want to fight with him. I held his hand, and we took some pictures, mostly of him in various poses – looking at the lavender, smelling the lavender, laying in the lavender, and jumping straight up out of the lavender with arms in the air like some kind of ad for soap. I have become quite adept at capturing the form of leaping Chinese boy in my shutter.

"Am I handsome?" he crooned. "I'm hot, right? I think I'm hot."

Other couples and photographers milled around, but only noticed us long enough to ask us to move out of their frames. I wondered if any of them stopped to think that we too might be a couple, with as much history and intimacy as any of the cookie cutter brides and grooms stomping around in formal wear. But most of them, like us, were just looking at the flowers.

The Mountain Spirits are Laughing

On the trail in Yunnan

Jeremiah Jenne

Day one

I AM BARELY surviving Shangri La. I'm standing on an observation platform 15,000 feet above sea level, on Jade Dragon Snow Mountain in Yunnan province. Known to the local Naxi people as Satseto, the mountain rises to over 18,000 feet and has only been summited once. I am in no shape to climb anything today and instead ride the gondola up. Just two days before I was in Beijing, and I am adjusting poorly to exertion at altitude. It takes a very specific act of concentration to not lavishly shit myself with every step.

Today is only the first day of a weeklong trek. I am hiking with a diverse group of fellow travelers, most of whom are significantly fitter than I am. The early spring weather is agreeably cool during the day, but I know that when the sun goes down behind the mountain the temperature will fall dramatically.

Of all of China's regions and provinces, Yunnan has always been my favorite. One of the most ethnically diverse and ecologically rich areas in all of Asia, sharing borders with Vietnam, Laos and Burma, Yunnan is a delight to the senses. Right now, I'm mostly sensing the onset of altitude sickness.

We return to Lijiang, a UNESCO designated city about an

hour's drive from the mountain. The Old Town was once the center of culture for the Naxi people, but what little Naxi culture existed before has been overwhelmed by tourism. Souvenir shops and cafés dominate the narrow cobblestone streets. The town's waterways are lined with music bars and discos advertise "cultural shows", featuring bored young men playing guitar or kittenish women in minority costumes dancing semi-chastely to bad music. It is as if the Lijiang city leaders and the local tourism development board have a vision, and that vision is to transform this world heritage site into Yunnan's answer to Branson, Missouri.

Lijiang is also one of several towns and cities in China and across Asia that claim to be the inspiration for James Hilton's 1933 novel Lost Horizon, which gave rise to the legend of Shangri La. It is for sale in almost every bookshop. While culturally speaking the tourist trap of Lijiang could not be further from a mystical mountain kingdom, the scenery of the surrounding area – deep forests, rocky gorges, snowcapped mountains – makes the idea less risible. Nearby is Tiger Leaping Gorge, a narrow canyon with walls rising thousands of feet from the riverbed to glaciated peaks above. The Jinsha river, a tributary of the Yangtze, rushes through the cool interior of the gorge with such force that it is considered unrunnable by white water rafters.

This corner of Yunnan was first made famous in the 1920s by the writings of Austrian-American botanist and explorer Joseph Rock. Yunnan was a very different place back then. The terrain that took Rock and his porters days or weeks to cross can now be traveled in hours. At the same time, it's hard to feel too sorry for him. While he endured bandits, bad roads, steep climbs and uncharted territory, he did so with a certain style. His train of porters carried boxes of scientific equipment, bed linen, and even, it is rumored, a working phonograph player.

Not all travelers come to Yunnan for the landscape. Every mention to my Chinese male friends that I was heading to Yunnan elicited a leering response and not-so-thinly veiled references to the exotic willingness of Yunnan minority women to bed strangers. To say that they have only the flimsiest grasp on the culture and practices of Yunnan minorities is generous. Minority groups in China, 26 of which live in Yunnan, are at best treated by the media as exotic and sensual primitives, and at worst as simpletons to be exploited. There is a lucrative business bringing men from China's cities to Yunnan on multi-day "Bang a Minority" tours.

At night I sit in one of the music bars in Old Town. The numbing effects of Beer Lao are a poor match for the thunderous techno being played on broken speakers. The historic district of Lijiang was almost completely destroyed in a 1996 earthquake. When it was rebuilt, most of the local residents found it more lucrative to rent out their old dwellings to shop owners, and the result was the steady commercialization of the town center. Now Naxi culture exists as a performance and a trinket. It is a fate sadly shared by many of the "Old Towns" I have visited in China and Asia, but the process has been grossly accelerated in Lijiang over the past decade. As I finish my beer and watch a team of models dressed in Carlsber" beer uniforms parade through the crowd, it is easy to convince myself that it's time to move on.

Day two

Five hours drive north of Lijiang, we arrive in Napa. I am disappointed to learn that there will be no wine tastings and that this Napa refers, depending on the season, either to a beautiful lake adorned with migrating cranes or a large muddy flood plain covered in yak shit. It is the dry season and the lake has disappeared. Instead of cranes, yak-cattle hybrids move slowly across the damp pasture.

I'm sleeping in the guesthouse of one of the villagers. Napa is a one-street village of about fifteen or so houses on the shore of the lake. The town is a peaceful place to spend a few days and a much needed respite from the tourist hordes of Lijiang. Children play in the fields. Industrial-sized Tibetan mastiffs wait patiently chained to gates, choosing to ignore the smaller dogs circling them like gnats buzzing around a bull's ass. The residents gather at sunset by the lakeside to gossip and argue.

At the far end of the village, the local residents have built a small hydro-powered prayer wheel that will spin for as long as there is water in the stream. It would be a scene of bucolic charm but for the garbage. All the most beautiful scenic spots in China are blighted by rubbish heaps. Rural villages are now within easy reach of the global market, and plastic and paper packaging is the colorful vanguard of consumer choice. But that market often extends into places that are still beyond the reach of public sanitation, and so the back fields and streams of China's countryside fill steadily with the multi-colored detritus of consumables.

There are other changes too. In recent years, residents in Napa and the other lakeshore villages have shifted their livelihood away from yak herding supplemented by quasi-legal logging to eco-tourism supplemented by quasi-legal tollbooths. At intervals along the highway separating the village and the lake, the locals have erected a makeshift barricade demanding between 30 and 50 yuan for vehicles to pass. It occurs to me as I watch the toll booth operators swarm a luckless SUV that this isn't so much a new practice as a reversion to type. The writings of Joseph Rock lament that highway brigandry has long been a staple of the local economy.

My host for the evening is the head of the tollbooth scheme, and at night he talks about his adventures waylaying passersby for money, while chain smoking cigarettes through a three-foot metal bong. I ask him if what he is doing is, in the strictest sense, legal. He scoffs and goes off on a rant about how the government built the road to facilitate tourism, but where is the money really going? Shouldn't the villagers get a share? It occurs to me that what he thinks of as "his share" would in other contexts be defined as "ransom", but I want to be a good guest.

Day three

I have stepped on a yak. Not yak dung, which has become such a part of my daily existence as to no longer merit comment. I have stepped on an actual yak, and the yak isn't happy about it.

Rural residents in this part of Yunnan live in two-story homes fronted with an enclosed courtyard. Generally, the family sleeps upstairs and the animals sleep downstairs. We are guests and so are sleeping in a blockhouse on the western edge of the courtyard. The privy is on the eastern edge, requiring, when nature calls, a short but perilous journey across the yard. It is dark and my headlamp is out of batteries.

Shuffling across the courtyard, I stumble over a large bulky shape, a sensation not unlike walking into a pile of sandbags. I have little time to identify this obstacle when the shape rises, knocking me backwards into a large puddle. The yak is not amused and lets me know so in no uncertain terms.

I grew up in semi-rural New England and part of me – the part not sitting in a puddle of mud and animal excrement – is pondering the irony of my having been just tipped by a cow. In a land where Buddhism runs deep, one ignores the possibility of karmic retribution at great cost.

Day four

On our way to Sichuan, we have stopped at Ganden Sumtseling Monastery. For nearly three centuries, this massive complex has been the largest and most important Tibetan Buddhist monastery in Yunnan. Originally founded by the Fifth Dalai Lama in 1679, it has survived rebellions, wars, and (barely) the Cultural Revolution.

Inside the main hall is the scent of Tibet: yak butter candles and incense. The atmosphere is thick, almost unbearable in the smaller chambers. Walking through doors the smoky air parts like a curtain. As with many Tibetan monasteries, the interior is darkened. We pass rows of icons, each with their own collection of offerings: mostly yak butter, but also money, fruit and other small gifts. In the corner of the hall sits an old monk. He looks as if he came into being as part of the hall when the structure was still new. He offers to sell me a small amulet.

"How much?" I ask.

"500 yuan."

"Just for the amulet?"

"Yes. For the amulet. But I can bless it for you. This will give you great fortune on your journey."

"How much does the blessing cost?"

"Depends on how much blessing you need."

I am still ignorant of the power of a monk's blessing and parsimonious with my budget. I politely decline his offer. This, I will soon learn, is a mistake. When dealing with the spirits of these mountains, one needs all the help one can afford.

Day five

On our way out of Napa, we intentionally bypass the town of Zhongdian. Another claimant to the mantle of "the real Shangri La," the town was officially renamed Shangri La in 2001 by craven local officials eager to siphon tourists north from Lijiang.

Sadly, a large part of the Old Town of Zhongdian burned in 2014 when a fire engulfed most of the town center. As with

Lijiang, when disaster strikes it is often the oldest structures which suffer the most and are the least likely to be saved. In their place arise the staples of all Old Towns throughout China: tacky shops with indigenous crafts lovingly "handmade" in factories in China's coastal cities; insufferable music bars; and the ubiquitous outposts of American junk food imperialism – KFC, Pizza Hut and a Starbucks or three.

This approach to historic preservation baffles many outsiders, but it's perhaps reflective of different attitudes between international visitors to China and domestic Chinese tourists. Generally speaking, international travelers come to China to see it as it was (or as they think it was). They crave authenticity. The actual. The real. No matter if that actual or real is dirty, old or in a state of decrepitude bordering on the structurally unsound. Chinese travelers prefer to see places as they should be or could be. They have little patience for dusty beams and broken stones. Many find gaudy reinterpretations of historical sites – and the shopping, dining and entertainment options which surround them – improvements on the original, and are genuinely puzzled as to why their foreign friends feel a photo of a rundown building or dusty alleyway is a better representation of China than a gleaming new historic site with a snack bar and souvenir stand. Such was the fate of Lijiang, Zhongdian is next, and we move on swiftly.

The border between Yunnan and Sichuan is wild territory of high mountain passes, and it has been snowing heavily since we left the monastery. Drivers in rural China tend to operate under the assumption that any road has the potential to be a Formula One course, and set their speed accordingly.

Our driver in Yunnan, safe in the irrational power of happy thoughts, seems oblivious to the possibility of imminent demise. The mountain roads are narrow and not quite one-way, but most vehicles avoid the perilous edge and stay close to the center of the road. This means that any curve or bend has the potential for a sphincter-shrinking encounter in which each vehicle swerves at the last second to avoid a head-on collision. This is immediately followed by another swerve to steer away from either a jagged rock face or a thousand meter drop.

By the second or third near miss, I am openly white knuckling the dashboard. Our driver seems amused at my discomfort. He gives me a big thumbs up before taking both hands off of the wheel to light another cigarette.

Day six

I dub thee Motherfucker Ridge. It is, apparently, inappropriate to refer to any part of a sacred mountain as "motherfucker". Even more so when on a kora, a circumambulation of a holy place. In my defense, I have lost count of the ridges I have crossed today. My fellow hikers, most of whom are significantly younger and fitter than I am, are nowhere to be seen. They are almost certainly already in camp ahead, resting.

I am sure this is the last ridge before camp, and when I see it isn't and I let fly with the expression of my displeasure and rage. In doing so I have called down the vengeance of angry mountain spirits. And it has been my experience that mountain spirits, when unnecessarily riled, can turn any trip into a fiasco – especially when you have blithely ignored offerings of spiritual aid from a helpful monk.

When I stumble into camp two hours later, I am sweating profusely in the cold mountain air, breathing heavily, and the rest of the group recoil from me as if approached by an apparition of death. My heart is pounding arrhythmically against the walls of my chest. I would vomit but I already lost lunch on the downward slope of Motherfucker Ridge, no doubt incurring additional penalties from the gods. I look and feel like I'm one bottle of tequila and two Mexican hookers away from reenacting the last five minutes of Chris Farley: The E! True Hollywood Story.

By night I am in a tent. It is quiet on the mountainside but I can't sleep. A thin pad provides little buffer between my aching muscles and the cold earth. Periodically, my legs cramp savagely, leading to a whimsical few minutes thrashing about on the floor of my tent while I try to straighten my seizing limbs. I am clearly not drinking enough liquids, even though I was told on several occasions that this was essential.

In my defense, to the extent that yak butter tea is a liquid, I did try to stay hydrated. The first cup was pleasantly warm and creamy on a cool mountain evening. A bit like a rich cocoa, except salty not sweet. The second cup was ... okay. The third gave me a tepid, heavy sensation in my stomach, as if I had just chugged a quart of recycled motor oil. There was no fourth cup.

The mountain spirits are having fun with me. I should have bought the damn blessing.

Day seven

We leave after a breakfast of fried eggs and porridge. I am guzzling warm water to keep my legs from cramping. I assume it's been boiled but I am beyond caring.

Luckily we are circumambulating the massif, not climbing to the summit. Summiting holy mountains of Tibet is not recommended as it is one of the surest ways to anger the mountain spirits. Since most of the peaks are challenging technical climbs carrying sufficient risk of avalanche, rock fall and crevasses, adding the wrath of vengeful deities seems like a bad idea.

Even from the shoulder of the mountain, the view of the summit is magnificent. Plumes of snow blow from the peak, an enormous white banner underneath a crystal sky. I am ashamed of my blasphemy the day before.

We pick our way along well-worn trails and over boulder fields born of landslides. As we cross by an alpine lake, we see a dozen local villagers carefully checking under rocks and in crevices.

"Chongcao," says our guide.

He means Ophiocordyceps sinensis, caterpillar fungus. This grisly plant attacks the larvae of certain moths. Once infected, the fungus paralyzes and then kills its host before sprouting a small stalk. Found only at high altitude, caterpillar fungus is famous throughout Asia for its medicinal properties. It is prescribed as a cure for a staggering array of maladies, from cancer to heart disease, but its alleged effectiveness in male enhancement is the main reason why this strange plant can fetch prices as high as $80,000-$100,000 per pound.

With that kind of money at stake, during picking season villages go all in on the collection and trade in caterpillar fungus. Locals spend their whole day carefully combing the mountainside looking for gold dust in the form of a mummified worm, the Viagra of the Himalayas.

Day eight

We arrive at a small monastery near the base of the mountain. The monks greet us and show us around. It is brighter and cheerier than the massive Ganden Sumtsaling, but there is still the unmistakable pungency of yak butter and incense in the air.

As we enter the main hall I am surprised to see an old monk sitting in the corner. Of course it can't be the same monk I met at Sumtsaling, but in my dehydrated, addled state of mind I can't be sure anymore. He greets me with familiarity and offers to sell me an amulet.

"Will you bless it?" I ask.
"Of course. For a donation."
"How much is the donation?"
"How much of a blessing do you require?"
I open my wallet and hand over the entire contents.
"I need you to undo a curse."
I think I can hear the mountain spirits laughing.

RICE FIELDS

Poetry

____

Tom Mangione

He sat in the car thinking

(this is how I've come to China
where ducks and dozers vie for space
in the muck and mud of paddies
where workers throw their backs down
among the rings of factory fanfares
calling the age to order
when men in collars or coolies
look upon each other and say
so neat, so straight
so perpendicular perfect:
"who will you be, how will you show
the time is now, our lives must grow"

grow on like mine too
grow on in this promise
of something new

beyond the dreams of decadence
of road-head seat-back love affairs
terminating in parking lot burgers

and marriage mortgage vows
the grail of garages
stabled with SUVs
to cart the fridges full
for foraging to the swish of soccer sacks
and clatter of cleats
that grow to thumping drums
and microphone wails
power-chord riffing
and silent reefer sales

then through the trouble
of my child's youth
to send them off
and hope to see them grow
beyond parties of ice-luged booze
and callithumpian orders
in books and letters
so neat, so straight
so perpendicular perfect:
"who will you be, how will you show
the time is now, your life must grow"

where my child thinks it too
to grow on in this promise
of something new

but I'll look at myself
worn and grayed before a mirror
like a veteran wolf
catching a glimpse on an icy riverbank
after several rounds

of beer-toting, good times
with buddies and babes from my past
in neck-gripped horror
before my dilated eye
I'll look back and say
I never grew
but stayed the same way

and so here is China
the land where revolution
cut a culture
deeper than the Marianas Trench
where words are stories
that whisper the rise and fall of life
that adorn this raised stretch of road
calling over our memories
from the green-grown past
to the skies of vacant condominiums
and salacious shopping malls
harbingers for what the world that will be
when concrete covers all I see
and everything I ever knew)

about rice fields.

Back and Forth

A short story

—————————————

Aaron Fox-Lerner

THE FIRST TIME I saw Fang Zheng, he was destroying a park full of old men. One after the other they would step up, and he'd humiliate them in turn. He didn't play down or patronize them. He never slowed his speed. They'd all watch as he dispatched them as fast as possible, his face showing a kind of malicious calm as he cut them down with rapid-fire arm strokesAs strangers go, he was an odd one. Dude practically reeked Chinese countryside. His hair had clearly grown out from a sheered buzz cut, his skin was dark and lined, hands big and rough, teeth arranged like cars in a junkyard. His clothes looked like they'd been rejected from the dollar bin; I was surprised that his plain slacks didn't split under his quick movements. He had one of those utilitarian striped canvas bags ubiquitous among migrants tossed off to the side near the ping pong tables.

The only incongruous part of him was the shoes. They were a pair of Butterfly sneakers, specifically made for playing table tennis. They were old and scruffy, but I could tell he'd taken good care of them. From the way they seemed weathered without being destroyed I surmised they were the real thing and not a cheap knockoff. That clearly made them the most expensive part of his outfit.

He used them judiciously. He didn't react too soon and didn't move if he didn't have to. Instead he lunged and swung in quick flashes, like a predator spotting fleet-footed prey. His form was all economy, as if he considered unnecessary movements an indulgence. He didn't see me until he was done with the old men. I'd been watching for a while by then.

When he saw me he just stared. I'd get this sometimes from migrants on the ever-crowded Beijing subway, basically the only time I'm forced into close proximity with them. They'd gaze at me, literally open-mouthed, fascinated by the foreigner standing right in front them, acting like I was a snow leopard that had just strolled onto line 10 with all the other commuters.

As far as I could tell this was what migrants did – come to Beijing and stare at things. It was like they'd led entire lives without the agency or ability to do anything but look on dumbly.

Fang Zheng was staring at me in that migrant way. He was clearly right off the boat, I thought to myself. Or well, not boat, but the hard seat section of an overnight train or bus or back of a truck or however these migrants actually got to Beijing. After a little bit I couldn't take it any more.

"Your ping pong is very good," I told him in Chinese.

He just stared at me for a beat before asking me what country I was from. I told him I was from Canada and he asked if that was part of America. I told him it was close. I have to admit that a little part in the back of my brain was disappointed that he didn't make more of a fuss over the fact that I spoke to him in Chinese. I started grilling him about his ping pong skills, which he also wasn't super effusive about. I asked him how he put that kind of spin on the ball and he just told me that he hit it well. Then he stopped. Something seemed to hit his mind and he suddenly took on a look suggesting a certain amount of guile, the first I'd seen from him since he started talking to me.

"Do you play ping pong?" he asked.

"Yes, but I'm not very good," I demurred.

He didn't care. He pressed me with a grin and a narrowing of his eyes. He insisted. He decimated me 11-0. I knew I never stood a chance but I still had to marvel at how concisely he cut me down. We stood there afterward and I asked him what the hell he was doing here.

"Playing ping pong," he told me. "Beijing is my country's capital. I want to play against the best. No one in my village can play ping pong well."

"And, uh, where exactly are you from?" I asked him.

"Shanxi," he told me.

"Oh, so pretty close."

"I guess," he said, "it took me a long time to get here. China is so big! I had to take a bus and then a train. I haven't taken the train since I was a little boy and today was the first time I've ever ridden the subway. It's so clean!"

After this he was silent. I stood there and looked at him and he stayed still by the ping pong table. He didn't look like he planned to move anytime soon. Finally I felt I had to break the silence.

"Where are you staying?" I asked him.

"Some people on the train gave me an address where I could rent a bed, but I don't know where it is."

I looked at the paper he had. The instructions included the nearest subway stop and then the address from there. It was way out by the fifth ring road.

"Jesus," I said, "that's real far out there."

"Wow," he said, "you know where it is?"

"Yeah, look, you want some food? I wanna get lunch."

"I don't think I can afford Western food," he said.

"No, no, it's on me. And I was just thinking cheap Chinese anyway."

He hefted his bag and we walked off to the snickers of the old men behind us in the park, joking over the country bumpkin wandering off with the crazy *laowai*. He didn't even seem to notice their derision; he just loudly introduced himself as Fang Zheng, over-explaining the two characters that made up his name.

I took Fang to a standard place down the road and ordered us some dumplings and spicy chicken. He goggled at the food and said I'd ordered too much. He asked me if I knew how to use chopsticks. I wasn't very interested in explaining to this guy that I was acquainted with basic aspects of Chinese culture. I wanted to know how this otherwise unprepossessing migrant ended up being such a killer ping pong player.

He insisted to me that there wasn't anything to talk about. He was just good at ping pong. That was it. He'd played it since he was a little kid, and he'd always been good at it. They all said so: other kids, his parents, the people at school. They'd even sent him to train. They thought he could be in the Olympics. But he didn't make it to that level of training, and by the time he was eleven or twelve he was just back at his school, playing for the school team and nothing else. He never even got to leave the province, he said.

So there I had it, nothing special. Wasn't even admitted into a national-level training program. A couple of bad games. He messed up under pressure. But he kept playing ever since, kept training, kept practicing, just by himself, whenever he could. But it was too late for him now. He was too old to be a real athlete. He worked in construction, where he used his lithe form and ingrained precision to scale bamboo scaffolding and thread wires.

That was it then, he was just an almost-ran. I said that he must have come here to work, then. No, he insisted. He'd come here to play ping pong. He'd come to Beijing to play ping pong and then die.

This last part required some clarification for me. He took a breath and looked at me.

"I was working one day," he said, "and I just looked up and thought my life has no meaning. I do not like my life. My job is very hard. I cannot find a wife. But I play ping pong well. I am 31 years old. Soon my ping pong will get worse, and I will have nothing. I decided I will come to Beijing, the capital, and play ping pong. I will try to defeat the best players I can find. This is the capital, there must be great players here. I will play as much as I can, and when I have played all that I can, I will be done. Then I can die."

"Are you serious?" I asked him.

"I want to do what I am good at. Nothing else. I have no other reason to live. These dumplings are okay."

"So you just want to play champions?"

"No, I'll play anyone. As many people as I can."

Growing up in Montreal, ping pong was something I viewed on the same level as tetherball or air hockey, a game to pass the time when bored at summer camp. Back then if I'd met someone who'd devoted his life to ping pong I probably would've just laughed at him. But when I went to Taiwan to study Chinese, I started hanging out with some Taiwanese kids who were also obsessive ping pong players. I ended up going along to their weekly basement ping pong club and found myself hooked.

I've never risen above the level of amateur, but it's a sport I've continued to enjoy. When I moved to Beijing a couple of years ago to work for a wine distributor, I started up another ping pong club. Most of the other players are also foreigners; ping pong for them is a light little way to have a Chinese experience, like buying an old Flying Pigeon bike or living in the *hutongs*. The few Chinese people in the club are pretty casual players too. They're basically the Mainland equivalents of my Taiwanese friends, the kind of people likely to not just speak passable English but to know the difference between New York and DC hardcore punk scenes.

I had no idea how they'd receive Fang Zheng, but I knew I'd lucked out in finding him on Wednesday, the day we played.

Once we got off the subway, he wouldn't stop gawking at the buildings in Sanlitun, but this changed when we entered the ping pong hall. His gap-toothed gape had closed into a tight, pursed line; his eyes had also narrowed into parallel determined marks. I could see him scanning the hall as if searching for the best targets.

The only people there were a group of high schoolers. They were good. Clearly part of a school team, quite possibly local champions. Fang walked right up to their table and watched intently as they played. They kept playing as if oblivious to his presence. He kept on staring, not a migrant stare this time. He looked like a swordsman about to challenge a rival dojo. He stood still, almost magisterial, tensed eyes barely displaying the fact that they were closely following the game, right up until one of the high schoolers beat the other 21 to 18.

The minute they finished he blurted out: "I want to play."

The high schoolers finally looked at him.

"Do you even have a paddle?" One of them asked him.

"In my bag," he said, already walking over to get it.

"All right," the winner of the last game said, "I'll play you."

The teenager was smiling as he said this. It wasn't really a superior smirk or anything. I could tell that this kid just thought he was doing something fun and a little odd by playing against this random stranger. Fang carried a very slight smirk too. He walked up to the table and told the winner that he could serve, no warm up.

The kid served.

The ball shot back and spun off the kid's side of the table, ricocheting towards the proprietor's desk.

The kid cocked his head like a cat before picking out another ball and sending it towards Fang with a ton of spin on it. Fang's arm shot out and the ball was back at the edge of the kid's side, bouncing off it, the kid was running for it, his arm swung out, and he connected, sent it back, but he'd run too hard, it had no control, and it went too far out, past Fang's side, onto the ground. Fang didn't even move as the ball shot past him. His eyes were on the kid. The tightened lips of his mouth moved up slightly.

The kid returned two of Fang's serves, and one time he almost started a volley, returning the ball a full two times, but that was all. Five of Fang's serves and the game was now ten-zip. The kid had lost any hope of coming back, but you could tell he was trying to score at least one point. He cut a risky shot to the side of the table ... and overshot. Fang moved slightly before letting the ball dive to the floor.

"Good game," he said, "who's next?"

The kids were interested now, in the way that young men throw themselves into tests of endurance. They all wanted to play Fang, more as an act of competition against each other than against him.

He stood at his end of the table and let them come against him one by one, taking them down in turn, the same cruel gleam in his eye from before. The kids lost to him in a steady stream, comparing their games amongst themselves as they watched the next competitor. One of them, a lanky kid with a bowl cut, actually scored a point on him with an unexpected (possibly fluke) return. The bowl cut kid was practically a hero after that.

Finally there were no more high schoolers to play. Fang looked around the room. A couple of my friends had arrived at the club, and that was it. The proprietor, who had started watching the matches intensely, finally decided to hobble over. He was an old man, small and bald, but not unhealthy-looking for his age.

"Who have you been training under?" he asked Fang.

"I haven't trained under anyone for a long time," Fang said, "I just play on my own time."

"You're not from here."

"No, Shanxi. Do you know where I can go to play the best ping pong players? I want to play the best there are."

"Do you have a phone number? I know some trainers, they might want to have you play against their athletes."

"Uh, I don't have a phone right now."

"I've got a phone," I said, "you can just use my number."

They both looked at me before agreeing to this. The proprietor said he would try to call or text me tomorrow. We waited as a few more people trickled in for the club.

Until he started to play, everyone was confused about what Fang was doing here. Li, one of my Chinese friends, complained to me that Fang kept asking him dumb questions about how he knew so many foreigners. Mostly people just stared at him as much as he stared at us. There was a good deal of giggling.

Once he started playing them, people's attitudes changed. They were no longer dubious of his presence, but came up to congratulate me on finding him, as if I'd just discovered a great party trick. They talked about him more like a well-trained animal than a skilled athlete.

After the club ended Fang took out his paper with the address on it, but I just told him he could just sleep on my couch. Most people had left, but Li was still hanging around and I could see him stiffen as I said this.

Li came up to me, his blue Sonic Youth washing machine t-shirt still clinging to him with sweat, and asked me if I knew what I was doing. He told me that I couldn't just trust anyone here. I know, I know, I told him. It would be fine. I took Fang back with me, made him take a shower before letting him sleep on my couch, and went to bed hoping I didn't wake up to find half my apartment gone.

I didn't, which was nice. I did, however, wake to find Fang just sitting there perfectly still like a decommissioned robot, which was creepy. He complained that it was late and he wasn't sure what he was supposed to have done while I slept. It was 8:30 in the morning. I fixed him some breakfast and then hit my real problem after we ate. What the hell was I supposed to do with this guy until I got the call from the proprietor?

I had some stuff to take care of at the office, but I wasn't supposed to be there until the afternoon. By 10 a.m. I couldn't take it anymore and just went into work early, kicking Fang out of my place and setting a meeting point for later that evening. The previous day had carried the excitement of discovery, but with that out of the way I couldn't think of a single thing to talk to him about.

Later, once he was out of my way and I was at work I got a call from the proprietor who had found a game for Fang through a trainer in one of the universities in Wudaokou. The proprietor said he was a very high level coach and only worked with extremely promising prospects. The coach was apparently working with some kind of prodigy and was always looking for someone able to play against him.

I took Fang there that night. The gym was clean and well lit, with orderly rows of tables at which dozens of young boys and girls practiced drills with military rigor and intensity. Towards the back a trim middle-aged man was working with a long-limbed, round-faced teenage boy. You know how a river in its continuous flow can look like a single long solid object? That was the best way I could describe this boy's movements. He looked like motion was his natural state and the ball was just another part of his body, an extra appendage that always faithfully found its way back to his paddle and then across to the other side of the table again.

Fang had walked over by himself and planted himself uncomfortably close to the table. I couldn't hear what he said, but he started talking to the middle-aged man, who stepped away from the table. Fang was carrying his paddle in a plastic bag; he took it out and tossed the bag to the wall. Everyone else in the gym was wearing shorts and exercise shirts, but Fang was dressed as I'd seen him before.

I managed to hear Fang say that he didn't need any warm up and then the teenager served and the ball hung in the air before making an unexpected pirouette down towards the end of the table away from Fang. And then Fang was lashing out his arms in those rocketing movements of his. The teenager was right back on the ball, though, and for the first time I'd ever seen, Fang was now fully in motion, moving like the kid he was playing against, the two of them whirling around opposite ends of the table, pulsing out a rhythm in pushes and pulls, making the ball float and dive and jump and run across air and board.

The volley kept on until the kid finally managed to shoot the ball to the left and Fang overshot in trying to return it. The next point was a similarly intense volley, but also eventually went to the kid. Fang managed to get the next point but then the kid got two more. It was Fang's turn to serve, and it turned into another intense volley, this one sending both of them dashing farther out, but the kid finally scored on that one again, too.

I knew now that Fang was fallible. He was better than anyone I'd seen before, but he was still below a world-class Olympian. Fang didn't seem to notice though. He kept playing, undeterred by his apparently imminent defeat. I wasn't sure the score even registered for him. He was simply doing the only thing he was good at. When the two of them launched into yet another rapid-fire volley I got a glance of him, suspended in the air like a ball with perfect spin, his skin glistening, his eyes narrow and burning, his mouth slightly open and curved upwards. I saw him and finally understood what he did, that no matter what his life was like, nothing in it would ever be as worthwhile to him as these brief, flashing moments. I blinked, the ball landed, and he moved once more.

OVER THE WALL

Gifting a VPN for Father's Day

Mia Li

ONE WEDNESDAY IN early June my father called me at work and said, "I heard it's going to be Father's Day soon."

Alarmed, I sat up in my chair and tried to make sense of this. My father had always said that the invented foreign festivals were decoys imported from America to sell cakes and carnations to China's new middle class gullibles. Even still, in recent years it had become customary for Chinese children to buy their parents gifts on Father's and Mother's Day. Pressure from both Confucius and the consumer industry had become insurmountable, let alone guilt trips from mum and dad. Starting the year I got a job, each year my mother dropped hints about what gift she wanted (at least she didn't make me hand over a portion of my salary like some other Chinese mothers do). But my proud father would never ask me for anything, so I thought.

"I'd like to get you a gift!" I said, in what I hoped was the right response. "What would you like?"

"I'd like an Astrill account," he replied, not skipping a beat. "I need to get over the firewall."

Again, my mind scrambled to summon the right reaction as a filial child. My father, a 57 year-old small-time exporter of cheap Chinese goods, wanted for Father's Day to evade China's Internet censorship. Before I could warn him of the potential risks of political dissent, he continued, "Can you help me? I definitely need to climb the firewall to keep running my business."

My father is a natural businessman, although it wasn't obvious at the beginning. Born in 1957 to a commerce bureau official and a math teacher, he had always been good with numbers. But his generation didn't have much help in pursuing their interests, and limited options for their future. They were, as Party propaganda put it, "little screws" in the gigantic machine that constructed the People's Republic. Young people were told to "go where the motherland needs it the most", regardless of personal ambition. The Party appointed a position to each of the little screws, who must keep their part of the machine working or be tossed away like scrap metal. Dreams and wishes were luxuries it was best to forget about. The Cultural Revolution started just when my father was preparing to go to school. Education suddenly became the arena of political games. Factions battled like gladiators with flyers, posters and fists. With nothing else to compare it to, my father thought that was what normal school life involved – pledging to be loyal to whoever was in political favor. Ten years later the madness ended, and at the age of 19 my father left school having learnt "nothing", in his words. He was ready to work.

Back then the Party assigned jobs and salaries according to how long one had been working. The earlier you started working, the more food and clothes tokens you would get. My father got a job close to home at a state-owned factory in Jinan, the capital of Shandong province. The province had been assigned to produce and dye textiles for the nation. My father's factory, Jinan No.1 Textile Dying Factory, would print patterns on blank fabrics, which would then be cut up and sent to shops across the country. Housewives traded fabric tokens for them to make clothes and curtains for their family.

And so my father became a "little screw" in the machine that kept the People's Republic clothed (no nation is constructed naked). The process of bringing fabrics from the factory to the shops fascinated him. He wondered how it was decided how many rolls of each pattern to print, and how to know which one would prove popular. He took a night school degree in economics, and was promoted to be in charge of planning the production schedule. When the token system and the planned economy ended, my father helped his factory prosper even more in a market economy. In the late 80s, he set up its export connections in Japan and Korea.

He got married, had me, and became the first man in his neighborhood to own a Japanese-made stereo. Once he spent the equivalent of an average worker's monthly salary on one smart suit. It was a new era, and things were going well. Then one day in the mid 90s, everyone at the factory was laid off. China was privatizing most of its state-owned enterprises. Almost all of the workers were given a severance package and told to find employment elsewhere.

My father always joked that his generation was the one that had the carpet yanked out from under them at every stage of their lives. Schools were suspended when they were starting to study; jobs were taken away from them when they were starting their careers.

He left the factory, took its clients with him, and set up his own company instead. He exported whatever he could – textiles and clothes at first, then automobile parts, porcelain, chemicals and rubber, a foot soldier in the giant standing army of China's manufacturing and export industry. Whenever the newspapers report on the enormousness of China's foreign currency reserve, I think of tens and hundreds of thousand of fathers like mine, exchanging their sales revenue into yuan so they can pay for food, rent and out-of-pocket medical bills.

As my father grew older, his profit margin grew slimmer. In the last few years, he didn't even make enough over costs to pay the flat-rate taxes to keep his company legal. But he refused to admit defeat. At the age of 57, his career in e-commerce began.

He joined an online directory of Chinese exporters set up by Alibaba, the e-commence giant. Customers around the world clicked onto his website, and signed contracts to source goods from Chinese factories. He set up a Google mail account to keep in touch with his buyers. (He tried Yahoo email too, but the company's China operation folded.) Although Google and many of its services had been blocked since 2009, Gmail was so widely used in the business world that it was considered too important to block.

One day in May 2014, it took my father four hours to send an email to one of his clients. He didn't know what was wrong. He rebooted his computer, re-installed the operating system, and performed all the bug fixes he could think of. A few days later, he found out that the government had finally blocked Gmail, in anticipation of the upcoming 25th anniversary of the 1989 protests. Having advertised his email address, he couldn't afford to switch. "The Party makes life a survival challenge to weed out the weak," my father joked.

Weak he is not. After dodging disaster in the Cultural Revolution, the nationwide SOE lay-off and with high taxes for private industry, he was ready to jump over another wall obstructing his way. But this time, he needed my help.

I bought him the Astrill account and helped him to set it up. Besides using Gmail, he has also started to access blocked Internet content from all over the world. He reads Chinese language news sites from New York, Toronto, Japan and Taiwan. He watches documentaries on YouTube. He follows the Chinese editions of *The New York Times*, *The Financial Times* and the BBC. (When I asked what he thought of their China coverage, he replied, "Not in-depth enough.") He told me he felt a sense of freedom he had never felt before.

"It was the best Father's Day gift ever."

Roots and Leaves

A journey back to origins

Courtney Han

Six of us were driving to my dad's hometown. My eldest cousin, age forty-five, was at the wheel of his new Audi. I sat in the front seat, with three cousins and my five-year-old niece in the back. The car was brimming with opinions. My youngest cousin recently turned down a potential suitor that my Fifth Cousin's husband found in his *danwei*. Her rejection was subject to intense debate. Family doesn't let you get away with anything.

"But he's a bad singer," she protested. "What if we're invited to karaoke? He'll embarrass me."

The last time I saw Twelfth Cousin, she was trying to study abroad in Belgium. Now she was a loan officer at a provincial bank and contemplating marriage.

"Who do you think you are, Madonna?" said Fifth Cousin. "You're just like your niece." My other niece was already twenty-two. "Last month she turned down a guy because he didn't have double eyelids. The time before, it was bad teeth. I don't understand you young people. You're nearly twenty-five. Do you want to be left behind?"

Fifth Cousin's husband was a policeman. They married six months after they met, and now have a twelve-year-old son.

The air conditioning blasted away. We zoomed past restaurants, boutiques and convenience stores hawking shrink-wrapped sausage, yogurt drinks and newspapers. Typical countryside fare. First Cousin played a song and everyone began singing along, until Fifth Cousin asked who sang it. "Liu Xi," First Cousin said. "I meant *originally*," Fifth Cousin insisted. They began bickering.

I shifted uneasily in my seat. We were all here on my behalf, and I wanted everyone to get along. It was the first time for me to come here on my own. Several days earlier, I boarded an overnight train in Beijing to Taizhou and called my father from First Cousin's car the next morning.

"What are you doing there!" Dad exclaimed. I pictured him sitting on the sofa at home in California, his whole face crackling with pleasure and surprise.

"Don't give them too much trouble," he said. There was a pause. I could almost feel the ache in his voice. "But stay as long as you can."

My Dad grew up in a small fishing village about two hours northwest of Shanghai. His stories about his hometown sound more like Mount Olympus than a poor Chinese village with a flooding problem. According to him, nowhere else in the universe was the air as sweet, the trees as lush and the jade-toned water as beautiful as in the *laojia*.

I was born in Beijing, where my mother's family lived, and moved to the US when I was five. My father's experiences growing up in rural China were as different from my American childhood as a fish from a bird's. His colorful stories about playing midnight hide-and-seek in fields, yanking river eels out of mud holes, climbing trees to peek at bird nests – they never happened on my visits. Instead I was coddled, stuffed with exotic foods, and kept under strict observation.

By day, I often felt treated like a circus monkey:

Does she talk Chinese? Does she talk English? Speak! Say something!
You think you know an English word, Old Zhang?
Puh. You don't know nothing.
Okay, then go and say it.
Ha! She didn't understand it!
Ha! You idiot!

At night, I was plunked into ornate banquet rooms to dine with droves of beaming relatives I'd never met. The bacchanals were full of gags and laughs. If no liquor was spilled, no chair toppled, no red-faced man glassy-eyed and stumbling, then it wasn't a good party. "You probably aren't used to this over there in America," a distant uncle would holler over the din of smashing cups. "Here, the louder we are, the better!" Then a tiny dog would yip madly from the lap of one of the older women who always excused herself early to play mahjong.

At the women and children's table, we drank yogurt and plum juice instead of liquor, and nibbled at delicacies crafted from duck liver, pig trotter, and permutations of tofu. It was my duty to accept everything and eat, or else face a chorus of hospitable reprimands: *Chi! Eat! Is this food for decoration?*

Rumor got around that I adored crayfish, the local joy and pride. It was a deceit I probably created myself through some clumsy gesture of politeness. Crayfish thrived in the region's many streams and ponds, and to me, resembled mutant insects, with their long antennae, studded pinchers and spindly legs. Impressively well-armored, the only edible part of the whole creature was the tail. To eat one, you must decapitate it, suck out the yellow-green juices from its head, peel off its shell casing and gingerly locate the thin intestine that runs down its fleshy back. *This you must not eat,* my relatives warned, holding up a translucent white strand for me to see. *This will make you lose your stomach.* After many nights sitting in a wrecked banquet hall extracting intestines from a basin of crayfish, I came to the conclusion that force-feeding myself a delicacy my relatives couldn't afford and I didn't like to be a fitting definition of my family.

My time in the *laojia* felt like a test of whether or not I could fit into China. I failed every time. I began to think I had a choice: Either try and gain admission into a clan with whom I shared a name and a face, or turn the other way. I turned the other way.

After college, I found a job at a research nonprofit that sent me to a rural island in the Philippines. The job promised challenge, adventure and a sense of purpose to indulge my millennial idealism. I spent the ensuing four years billowing from place to place, mostly in developing countries. I chatted up farmers and fishermen in Cote d'Ivoire; rubbed elbows with trust fund children in Manila; and lingered in opulent hotel lobbies in India to dance in clubs I would never go to back home.

Wherever I went, I made an effort to embrace the traditions, befriend the locals and learn some phrases of the language. But on weekends, many of my expat friends and I relapsed into the brunch-and-cocktails safety net of our tribe. We built communities with dinner parties and weekend trips, but for most of us, it was temporary.

I'll never forget one rain-soaked night at a film screening in Nairobi, where several bright young Kenyans stood up when it ended and praised the filmmakers for making their country proud. The air vibrated with applause. Afterwards, I chatted with one of them, a towering man with a gentle voice, who told me: *The art scene in China must be wonderful.* I felt a twinge of sadness. He could not see me belonging to their art scene, and I realized I knew less about contemporary culture in the country I came from than the region where I now lived.

Well, I said, *I was born in China, but I'm actually from the US.*

He laughed. *So how did you get here?*

How did I get here. I thought I was here because of my desire to understand, and maybe one day to contribute. But why this particular path, of all possibilities? How did I become this person with this set of experiences and this bone structure? How did I come to make these choices that resulted in this life?

You can only run so far from yourself. China was as part of me as my hair and single-lidded eyes. I had inadvertently allowed myself to exist in neither East nor West by traveling everywhere in between, but by doing so I was postponing the task of deciding how to divide my identity between those two poles.

It took bouncing through more than thirty countries for me to realize that tending to my roots was just as important as extending my branches. A tree with a weak foundation faces stunted growth, just as a person without a strong sense of self struggles to develop into a fully formed adult. Understanding the journeys my parents and extended family took would give me greater context for my own journey, and help illuminate my path ahead.

I moved back to Beijing in November 2014, and lived in my late maternal grandfather's flat. The rooms felt smaller and dustier than my memories of the place from when I was five, but I could still breath in the rich aromas of *hongshaorou* from a nearby flat in the late afternoons; still walk in the same neighborhood park I grew up playing in; and still imagine my grandmother in the living room, watching her soaps. Winter went by, and then spring. The following summer, I finally felt ready to return to my dad's *laojia*.

Fifth Cousin leaned over me in the car and tapped on the window. "Look at those people."

It was early July, and the narrow concrete streets were covered with wheat. Several leathery farmers were slowly pulling rakes through the grains, as if brushing hair. "See how slowly they move? Not like you people in Beijing." She clucked her tongue. "We don't have to run around. We have breakfast, lunch and dinner, and we stare at the clock until time runs out and we go home."

She showed us pictures on her iPhone of her son and husband. "See our lives? Our lives are simple. Before we know it we'll be fat and retired, happily eating and drinking all day." My cousins all laughed and agreed.

I wondered if she would become like the old-timers in Xinghua, repeating circumscribed routines every morning: Meet friends at the teahouse at 6 am, have soaked tofu and hot tea over the morning paper; go to the park by 7:30 for a walk, and back at home in time for breakfast with the grandchildren by 8:15.

"It's so hot," Twelfth Cousin said. "We should have come earlier."

"We had a late night," First Cousin said gruffly. Last night's long, liquor-fueled family dinner went a long way to explain everyone's languor.

He turned to me. "Let me ask you. Do you think I like smoking?"

I hesitated, thinking of the plume of smoke that surrounded him last night at his home, when we sat up late to talk for several hours before he finally attempted a Rihanna lyric in his raspy smoker's voice and we called it a night.

"No?" I said.

"Yes. Right. *Very OK*." First Cousin had a habit of saying "Very OK" in English to emphasize a point. "I hate smoking. I don't smoke because I like it. I do it because it's polite. It's *tradition*."

"Did he keep you up half the night telling stories about how he kills snakes with his bare hands?" Third Cousin said. "He does that when he's drunk."

Suddenly we heard a squeal. I turned around to see my niece retching all over the backseat.

"Whoa whoa!" First Cousin cried. His car was nearly as precious as his son. He pulled over.

First Cousin produced a box of tissues from the backseat to sop up the mess. Third Cousin took my niece by the hand and pulled her out of the car, saying, "Why didn't you give us a warning?"

"Where are they going?" I asked. I watched them fade from the passenger seat mirror as we drove on.

"They'll walk. We're nearly there."

"It smells so bad back here," Twelfth Cousin whined, covering her nose with a handkerchief. "I think I'm going to throw up too."

"Don't you start. Everybody out! We're all walking!" First Cousin pulled the car into a lot of rusted ingots and parked over a patch of drying wheat. We got out, blinking hard from the bright hot sun, and headed towards the *laojia* on foot.

We bought reams of yellow, tissue-like paper at a convenience store and carried them through empty fields and over bridges. The cemetery was just across the river from the village. Most of my cousins were here in April during the Qingming festival, or "tomb sweeping day", when about eighty members of the family reunited for several days of feasting and paying respects to ancestors. Following tradition, they swept the family graves but now, just three months later, the cemetery was overgrown again with weeds.

"Where are the goats when you need them," First Cousin muttered.

"My dress is caught," Twelfth Cousin complained, wobbling in her platform sandals and trying to unhook her flowery dress from a thorny bush.

"I hate all these insects," Fifth Cousin said, swatting at gnats and mosquitoes.

Each grave consisted of a concrete mound that resembled a large, hardened anthill, and was marked by a tombstone. There were hundreds scattered across the riverbank. Many were topped with two inverted flowerpots, their bottoms touching. We found our grandparents' plot, made a clearing in front of the tombstone bearing their names, and began burning stacks of paper to send "money" to them in the afterlife.

The thick smoke made my eyes burn and soon all of us were sweating from the heat of the blaze. To move things along, First Cousin took charge. "Grandpa and Grandma, your grandchildren have come to see you," he announced. "And one has come all the way from America."

I met my grandparents a few times. We couldn't understand one another, because I didn't speak the local dialect. Grandpa fell when trying to air out winter blankets, and died a week later in 2005. Grandma outlived him by nearly a decade, but was blind and deaf through most of it. She spent many afternoons sitting in the village with her few surviving friends, cackling away at something only they understood.

"How are you doing on the other side?" First Cousin continued. "We miss you very much."

"I don't know how many times our parents told me about those days," Fifth Cousin said, smiling. "To think, she lived to see ninety. They were real survivors."

"Your grandmother spent her whole life raising not only her own kids but some of your extended family's too," Third Cousin said. "Your grandfather supported six children on ten RMB a month." That's less than two dollars today.

I imagined them receiving our paper emissaries. I saw my grandfather spending it on good cigarettes and liquor, my grandma on fatty pork belly. They had no reason not to indulge their worldly vices, now that they had crossed over.

"Everyone, kowtow three times," First Cousin directed us.

My cousins and I turned to the grave and got on our knees in front of the blackened mass of burnt paper. If any of them felt as self-conscious as I did, I couldn't tell. I bent over and dipped my head three times, then a few more for good measure.

"Your great-grandfather was a giant of a man," First Cousin said, as we made our way towards his grave, some fifty paces over. "He could pull a plow as well as an ox, and he ate a whole pot of rice for dinner. The Guomindang was afraid to pillage the village because of him. It's a pity our Grandpa took after his tiny mother. Right there, a whole genetic line – ruined!

"See that grave over there?" First Cousin pointed. "That's Grandpa's younger sister. He had a soft spot for her. I remember—" he stopped and chuckled. "I remember your grandparents fighting many times about her. Why are you so good to her when we don't have enough to go around, Grandma used to say."

"I didn't know that," Twelfth Cousin said.

"You don't go to enough family meetings," First Cousin said. "Look over there. That's your great-great-grandfather's brother's grave. Three of the five brothers are buried here."

I pictured strong brothers spending their entire lives together, now lying ten meters apart in death. They embodied the Chinese character *jia*, which doesn't distinguish between "home" and "family," because for them and millions of other Chinese peasants, family was home and home was family. I thought of the contrast to Chinese migrants today, my own itinerant life, and of my parents, uprooting themselves to relocate thousands of miles away in an alien land for the sake of a "better" life. I thought of my cousins, and my aunts and uncles, who had dispersed to cities and dreamed of sending their children far away to attend the best schools. It seemed that for all of us, family was growing further away from home.

The six of us walked through the village to visit to my grandparents' house. No one has lived there since Grandma passed away two years ago. The narrow streets, bleached bone white by the summer sun, were exactly as I remembered it. The courtyard, full of tiles and potted plants, with an outdoor sink and wood-burning stove, looked the same. The same watercolor painting of mountains and charging horses hung on the wall, with calligraphy poems running down both sides. I ran my fingers over the white bust of Mao next to old liquor boxes and green tea tins on the table, and tried to picture my grandmother in her favorite reclining chair, which was now collecting dust.

We studied the family photos on the living room walls. I saw familiar faces at spring festivals, weddings and funerals in the images. There was First Uncle as a young man in his soldier's uniform, his smooth, unlined face handsome and doll-like. Second Aunt in a red dress on her wedding day. And I even found me, standing with three of my cousins on another visit to the *laojia*, years ago.

There was weight to the space within that old house that I didn't feel in the apartments of my relatives in the city, with their cheap plywood floors and flimsy furniture. Perhaps it was because things back then were built to last, while today, they are made to adapt to change. Or perhaps it was the accumulation of so many moments over the years — of joy, pain, sorrow, laughter. Perhaps it was these moments that now lived in the sturdy wood beams and fortified the house with special strength.

I took photos. I sat in the chairs. I lingered with my eyes shut for so long that when First Cousin said "Shall we go?" I thought I had imagined it.

There's a Chinese saying, *luoyeguigen*: "A falling leaf returns to its roots." It means all things go back to their source, as people return to the homes and countries of their birth. I'm one of the lucky ones – I can always return to my *laojia*. But it doesn't make leaving it any easier. For my cousins, this house is part of their childhood, little more than an abandoned house with our family pictures on the wall. But for me, it is one of the few remaining threads I have to the world I came from. This is family; this is home. I can sense its presence as well as its fragility. When I leave these doors, it will recede in my memory like a powerful dream that fades the next morning, or a haunting song on the radio that I won't find again. The only thing left of this visit will be an imprint that touches me but eludes my grasp.

As we head back to the city, the mood in the car is one of relief. My cousins are sleepy, and eager to get on with their weekends now that family duties had been fulfilled. I look around, and wonder where they will be next time I return. First Cousin has started his own business, growing wheat and rice and raising free-range chickens and pigs. Perhaps he will succeed in growing grapes, or purchase the pond across from his farm for the fishery he has always dreamed of. Fifth Cousin's tumultuous marriage has stabilized, and her son won second prize in the school art contest. Twelfth Cousin hasn't met her Prince Charming yet, but he'll be a damn good singer when she does.

My visits over the past fifteen years have been sporadic, but each time I gain a little more self-awareness. I am reminded that I'm not merely a daughter and sister in America, but a niece, cousin, aunt and now great-aunt in China. When I go back, I will encounter new additions and subtractions to the family ledger. We will celebrate the new arrivals and mourn the passed, and I will be reminded that no matter how dislocated I feel when shuffling from one place to another in this ever-shrinking world, there is a strain of continuity that runs within me. It is this family who links my past to my future, who nurture my roots and help me extend my branches.

Love, Anywhere

Fiction

Hannah Lincoln

THAT SUMMER, WHENEVER Wang Fei played guitar at Xiao Peng's bar, he made a habit of offering cigarettes to everyone in the audience. He took careful note of which girls did and did not accept. Most did not, at first. He would play two or three songs and then offer again. It didn't matter if they took it or not; the important thing was that they smiled at him.

Wang Fei would light their cigarettes, then his buddies', including Xiao Peng's, and finally his own. By then his glasses, which he had removed for the show, would be back on his nose, and he would lean in to clink beers all night until he was as scarlet as everyone else. Eventually Xiao Peng would drive them home on their electric bike.

Xiao Peng and Wang Fei had shared a university dorm for four years. After graduation, their group of friends had split across the country, settling into internships or graduate schools or their childhood bedrooms. Wang Fei considered himself too spiritual for an office job, too talented for his hometown. There was only Beijing.

For Xiao Peng, there was the internship at the bank that his father had helped him secure back home. But a week prior to graduation, Xiao Peng surprised everyone when he announced he was coming to Beijing as well.

"Stability's overrated!" was all he'd said to explain his decision.

Months into their Beijing residency, Wang Fei adopted the same attitude toward his once-imminent success as a rock star – it was overrated. He had yet to meet anyone in the record industry, anyone who hadn't stumbled across him belting out ballads at a handful of near-empty live music Houhai bars.

Wang Fei did not want conventional success, he decided – that could only be found by rubbing shoulders with those in power. He didn't want to pull *guanxi*, or do industry networking. He didn't want to spend greasy nights in bright banquet halls, pounding *baijiu* with jerk-off businessmen who had probably never even heard of Cui Jian. He was no sell-out.

Whenever Xiao Peng made some suggestion to Wang Fei – you can promote yourself on Weibo, you don't need to drink so much every night to prove you're an artist – Wang Fei said nothing in response. What did Xiao Peng know of dreams? He had no inspiration or ambition; he spent his days playing computer games in their apartment. Why else had he come to the capital if not to latch onto Wang Fei's dreams?

Most the time, though, Wang Fei didn't mind the company. Xiao Peng could be quite useful. He was often the only one in the audience of those blue-lit music bars or, if there were others, the first one clapping at the end of the songs. He always stayed sober enough to drive their electric bike back to their apartment. Then, just after New Year, Xiao Peng opened his own bar.

Wedged between a noodle shop and a dry cleaner, "Anywhere" barely squeezed itself into existence. It offered cans of beer and the contents of a few dusty liquor bottles lining a wooden shelf behind the bar. It was as if their dorm room from university had relocated to Beijing.

Xiao Peng found a bar counter, a foosball table, and a

collection of fraying wicker stools that he arranged around a small wooden stage designed for Wang Fei. For months Wang Fei sang his ballads to an audience of one until, gradually, the wicker stools filled with bodies. He handed out cigarettes seven nights a week to anyone who dropped by Anywhere. By the following summer, Wang Fei and Xiao Peng had started calling his modest group of fans "the faithfuls".

The faithfuls often showed up early, around dinnertime, with boxes of lamb kebabs in hand. Xiao Peng and Wang Fei ate with them until other customers arrived. Then Wang Fei's guitar appeared and Xiao Peng had to get to work.

A few times, Wang Fei talked one of the prettier faithfuls up on the roof where they could be alone. On the nights when that went well, Wang Fei himself drove the electric bike back to the apartment while Xiao Peng slept on the couch at the bar.

The last week of August swept through like a celestial sigh, the sticky summer pollution giving way to crisp starry-skied evenings. A literal shift in the winds was enough to make one fall in love in Beijing, the way it swept the *hutong* of its heat and scattered the cloud of smog.

It was an abnormally crisp and starry night when a girl in a long red skirt stepped onto the roof of Anywhere.

Xiao Peng sat her down at the end of the roof's long plastic table, diametrically across from Wang Fei and disappeared back downstairs. Wang Fei removed his glasses and extended a cigarette. She waved her hand no.

"Keep playing," she said. "Xiao Peng said you are very good."

"You're a friend of Xiao Peng's?"

"An old friend, yes."

How had Xiao Peng never mentioned this girl? Maybe he just didn't want to share. Wang Fei snorted under the rising notes of the guitar strings. Well, fine. Wang Fei had had his summer of success; why not let his friend have a taste?

And yet.

Wang Fei put down his guitar, shoved his glasses on, and grasped his phone and began to text his friend. Xiao Peng, how do you know this girl?

An old family friend, Xiao Peng replied. What's up? Can you tell she's a *Mosuo*?

Before he could type back Introduce me, her red skirt swished across the patio and stopped before him.

"Xiao Peng wanted to introduce me to you, but he's busy downstairs."

"Have a seat."

"I'm Lishuo."

"I'm Wang Fei."

"I know. Xiao Peng already told me about his musician friend."

"What did he say?"

She smiled at him. "I'm in Beijing visiting a cousin, but I said I'd come see how Xiao Peng is doing."

"And how is he doing?"

"Well …" she looked away and laughed. Wang Fei offered her another cigarette, and she waved it away again.

"Do you and Xiao Peng share an apartment?"

"Yeah, we've been living together for nearly six years now – since first year at university."

"I'd like to see it."

It's true what they say about *Mosuo* girls, Wang Fei chuckled. He knew better than to respond. Instead, he only carried on with his guitar for a while until she stood up.

"I've got to go."

"What?" Wang Fei was confused. "Will you come back

tomorrow?"

"We'll see."

When he woke up at noon the next day, on a mat across the sprawl of clothes and cups and electronics from Xiao Peng, Wang Fei had already received a message from Lishuo.

You will find true love on the roof of Anywhere tonight.

This is what she was like! Wang Fei was agitated all day, and then finally it was evening. He ordered Xiao Peng to rope off the roof; not even the faithfuls should be able to come up.

"Wang Fei, I don't think she's coming tonight," Xiao Peng said.

Wang Fei smirked, "Oh, she's coming. She told me."

The two of them sat listening to the babble and clinking bottles downstairs. Soon it was midnight.

Unable to stand it, Wang Fei sent Lishuo a message: I thought you said I could find you here.

Her reply came immediately: I said you could find love anywhere.

"She's standing me up, dammit!" He slammed his phone on the table and ripped his glasses off so fast they flew out of his hands.

Xiao Peng picked them up. "Wang Fei."

"What?"

Xiao Peng fiddled with the bent glasses but as much as he struggled could not make them straight.

"Wang Fei," he said, "Love isn't anywhere, it's here. Right now. Do you understand?"

Wang Fei shrugged and once again held his tongue. What did Xiao Peng know of love and rejection? He pulled out his phone and began to type madly.

Xiao Peng stood over him for a long time while Wang Fei

mashed away at his cell phone.

"Do you want a smoke?" Xiao Peng finally said.

"Yeah." Wang Fei did not look up.

Xiao Peng lit his own, threw the box onto the table, and disappeared downstairs.

Ramadan in Kashgar
A pilgrimage for dinner

Brent Crane

Unless you are in Xinjiang during Ramadan, as a foreigner you will never go hungry in China. Eating is a national obsession, and food takes on an almost sacred air. Cheap plastic table-top restaurants are everywhere, everyone is constantly talking about the next meal, and Chinese hosts will bend over backwards to make sure you've eaten enough. Often I'm confronted by a fierce jabbing of chopsticks in the direction of a half-finished communal dish and the barking command "eat!" delivered as the paragon of hospitality.

So I am surprised to find myself roaming the twisting streets of Kashgar's atmospheric old town, in furthest west Xinjiang not far from the border with Pakistan, with a rumbling stomach and diminishing chances of finding an open restaurant.

It is August 2014, right in the middle of the fasting month of Ramadan observed by Muslims all over the world, including by Kashgar's majority Uighur population. There isn't a square meal to be found. It feels like a deliberate famine. There is food to be bought, of course – sweet snacks at street stands, and instant noodle packets under two inches of dust on convenience store shelves. But I have lived off instant meals for the last three days, on the slow train from Gansu and already two months of journeying through China. My cells demand more satisfying nutrition.

It only makes matters worse that there are signs of food all around me: deserted kebab stands, empty noodle stalls, abandoned pieces of brass cooking ware. Inside boarded up eateries, chairs are stacked tragically on tables like the dusty ruins of a faded civilization.

In front of one street-side dive that is seemingly still open hangs a menu with aged photos of egg noodles, lentils and chunks of blackened lamb. Optimistically, I push through the green slats of plastic that shroud the doorway. It is the kind of small restaurant with tiny stools and tables, a pitiful plastic trash bin tucked underneath each one, that I have developed passionate feelings towards – a combination of nostalgic appreciation and deep-seated loathing. You never know if you are going to be met inside by a friendly face or a barking brute.

At the far end of the room sits the boss, a skinny man slumped lethargically at his table. Standing next to him, his wife is pale as an egg noodle, wearing a piece of lentil-colored cloth over a bun of hair the color of blackened lamb.

"Are you serving?" I ask the pair.

"No," the owner replies. He looks as if I have uttered the most imbecilic question of all time. "Don't you know it's Ramadan?" The wife stares longingly towards me, like I'm made of pure kebab.

"I know, but your door is open." He shrugs and brushes me off with a wave of his hand. I stomp out to resume my search in the full heat of the noontime sun. It is a sluggish, vitamin-deficient investigation.

But what am I complaining about? I came to Kashgar to find respite from the seeming cultural homogeneity of the rest of China. It is the only city I have traveled to that feels almost completely detached from what one normally thinks of as Chinese. Most of its inhabitants are Turkic, bearing little resemblance to their Han brethren. The men walk confidently, with a self-assured swagger that would make most East coast Chinese jumpy. The women wear headscarves and cover up their skin with pants and long sleeves, no matter how stifling the heat.

They are also a religious people, who refrain from alcohol and pork, the two main staples of the Chinese diet. Here, instead of pork there is lamb. You can spot the poor beasts tied up in droves outside sidewalk butcher stands, waiting dumbly in a queue for the chop, standing inches from the coagulating pools of blood drained from their slaughtered comrades.

A few days earlier, a friendly Turk I met outside the iconic Id Kah mosque, China's largest and oldest, asked if I wanted to witness the ritual. "Do you want to see them kill the lamb?" he asked plainly.

"Sure," I said and we walked ten feet over to the edge of the sidewalk, where a crowd of men had gathered to watch the killing. The butcher, a man not older than 25, wore a stylish striped t-shirt and jeans. He had no apron and grinned at the audience as he sharpened his knife. It felt like we were about to see a street magician.

"They must do it in the right way," the Turk explained. "So that it is *halal*, and good in the eyes of God." He said the last part in a very serious tone, in contrast to his initial boyishness.

"How do they make it *halal*?" I asked, as the butcher kneeled on the ground by the lamb.

The butcher hoisted the animal's head up by its chin. Everyone leaned in. "As he slices the throat, they will say 'In the name of God.'" He made a pretend cutting motion across his neck, and the butcher mirrored the motion with his knife across the neck of the lamb. "Then the animal will not feel pain." The creature's legs kicked futilely as it bled out.

"See! Look in his eyes, he is happy to be going to God!" the Turk said. The beast's eyes bulged widely. Joy was not an emotion I could find in them.

Absolutely starving, I sneak into the breaking-of-the-fast service at Id Kah mosque, that happens each evening during Ramadan when the sun goes down. I am on assignment, contracted by Al Jazeera to take photos of the holiday celebrations, and am feeling more intrepid than usual. As thousands of Uighur men pour into the mosque, I slipstream one of the groups in, my camera hanging from my neck, and make it inside without being stopped.

Inside, a line of famished-looking Muslims are resting on their knees before plates of food. They wear loose pants and breezy tunics. There are red apples, golden pears, Hami melon, torn pieces of bread, and slices of red watermelon. Next to the plates are upturned drinking bowls of neon green and blue. It looks mouth-watering.

Standing there, as men shuffle by to take their place in the seated food line, I feel more out of place than I have ever felt before in China. Blonde, tall and wearing shorts, I stick out like a heathen among the devout. Nearly everyone is glaring at me. I am used to being the center of attention in China, but I have never been the focus of so many people's gaze at the same time. It is as if the entire force of their faith, concentrated and empowered in these sacred moments, is aimed at me like a quiver of holy arrows. Finally one is released.

"Are you a Muslim?" a voice asks. I can't make out who spoke in the dying light, but it doesn't matter – the question is shared by the whole congregation.

"No," I admit, "I'm not." I wait for the boot but am greeted by silence. I interpret this as either listless indifference or congenial acceptance, and stand my unholy ground.

Feeling I should get out of the line of fire, I sit down on some steps to one side. The hungry chain of fasters continues unbroken along the walls to both sides of me, awaiting orders.

Soon, a man approaches to chat. He comes in peace. As we talk I feel relieved to have the morsel of legitimacy that speaking with this friendly insider confers on me. If the critics demand my exile, at least someone might come to my defense. But his Chinese is even worse than mine, and it's a stumbling exchange. I reach a peak of confusion when he hands me a can of scented aerosol spray – some unheard-of flower – which to the best of my knowledge I hadn't asked for.

The crackling of a loudspeaker interrupts our fumbling conversation, and everyone quiets down. The voice of the Imam booms over us and after some brief sermonizing he gives the go-ahead to gobble. The crowd spontaneously erupts in a voracious feast.

Watermelon juice dribbles down chins, breadcrumbs rain to the floor. Pits and peels are flung through the air into trash bins. Water is swallowed in great gulps. Not a single word is spoken during the whole affair. It is the quietest pig-out I have ever seen.

One man comes over to me with a handful of white peaches. He smiles like a drunken sailor and offers them to me. I wolf down the lot, tossing the slimy pits into a drain. They taste like a gift from God himself.

When the Imam's voice comes back on over the loudspeakers, all of the food is gone. The congregation stands up and walks towards the worshiping hall to face towards Mecca for the closing prayers. The night is quiet and the air is still. I snap a few photos and head out into the street to find some more food. I wasn't famished anymore, but I wasn't yet full.

EMEI CITY

A poem

Yuan Yang

The summer soon gone,
I was walking in my first hometown.

The guardsmen at the district gate
watched me like a stray white cat:

unthreatening.

When you have moved homes
like a fox moving dens,

to long for your original owner
is to forget you no longer

belong to an owner, and

yet, before feral,
you nosed your way back,

to the street filled at night
with the white smell of gardenias.

This morning, corn is burning
along the embankment.

The smoke brings a mixed nausea
for the many lives that go walking with me

down Emei River.

It trembles in the August morning:
slow ripples from dragonflies on the water.

The tremors pass and fill one another,
some higher, some lower, some left

yet stiller.

In the Hutong
The unbearable lightness of Beijing

Alec Ash

Mrs Wang the widow has lived on Xiguan Hutong for thirty-five years. She's an old Beijinger, born in 1951, and has been within a cabbage's throw of the same vegetable market for most of her life. Her childhood home was in Daxing Hutong, in the same block; her primary school was in Fuxue Hutong, two alleys down; her early teens were in Nanluoguxiang, back when it was just another residential ginnel. In 1980 she married a man who owned property in Xiguan Hutong (reinstated after the Cultural Revolution ended). She worked in a small factory five minutes walk away, making musical instruments from flutes to French horns. When her husband died four years ago, her son moved in with his Mongolian wife. Mrs Wang took a bedroom at the back to live out her retirement watching Chinese soaps, coddling her infant grandson and complaining about how her daughter-in-law complains about her.

There are fifteen households in the *dazayuan* or "mixed courtyard", which bends in an L shape from the street entrance behind the public toilets outside. The other landlords and ladies – all members of the Shi family, like her late husband – live off the premises, but Mrs Wang is an unmoving hub. The other residents change with every spin of the wheel. Some are young Chinese graduates, living on a budget in crumbling shoeboxes with no inside loo. There is one more nuclear family who own their property, the Xis. The rest are foreigners, mostly occupying the renovated building at the front with double-glazed windows and heated floors. Mrs Wang's neighbors have recently included a Czech, a Frenchman, a Mexican, two Russians, and a gaggle of Americans and Brits – though it's all about the same to her.

Ever ready with a toothy smile, Mrs Wang is indulgently curious about the foreigners. She doesn't approve that the Americans on the first floor are always bringing home girls, but otherwise finds them more polite to her than most of the old timers in the neighborhood are. She noticed that only she and one of the Russians, Maxim, keep the courtyard clean by sweeping it. When she spots the frizzy-haired bear of a Canadian coming home in the wee hours of morning, she wonders what he can possibly have been doing all night, or if he in fact gets up earlier than she does (answer: no). She never calls the police if there's a late night party. And she always stops to chat with the lanky Englishman who lives up the steps above, asking with fresh concern each time how old he is and if he's married yet.

When I arrived three years ago, in the autumn of 2012, Mrs Wang was just another stranger in an unfamiliar neck of the woods. I had lived in Beijing before – after graduating I served two years' hard time in Wudaokou learning Chinese – but I had worked in London for the past couple of years, and on returning found that much of China was new all over again. My then roommate, Pamela, had found the place, and I moved in on the same afternoon that I got off the Trans-Siberian train at Beijing station, having taken seven weeks traveling overland from England. I was just in time to catch the swansong of summer, and one last mahjong game outdoors.

My first impressions were of all the colorful clichés of *hutong* life. The couple who sold fruit and veggie on odd days at the street door, so I would have to step over a bucket of salty duck eggs to get out in the morning. The gourds and melons hanging from the vine, threatening to drop and knock out unsuspecting passers by. The man on the rooftop across from mine signaling with a red flag as his pigeons circled overhead, whistles strapped to their backs whining like a passing UFO. The lady who kept a pet dragonfly tied to a piece of string, to eat the last of the mosquitos. The hawkers' cries, clanging together knife sharpening rods or plaintively minstreling for second-hand furniture.

Xiguan means "narrow pipe", presumably after how the *hutong* starts off wide but tapers dramatically. Whenever a car mistakenly thought it could get through the pipe, I would silently curse it while stuck behind on my second hand racing bike. The city outside was constantly intruding. There was a large middle school just behind my building, and the students gaped out of their windows and into mine. Further down was a barracks for the People's Armed Police, who sometimes drilled through the alleys. But on lazy Sundays, I could avoid the main street all day long and imagine that I lived in a village. I made the effort to get my neighbors' surnames down. The local convenience store owner was delighted at my awkwardly formal way of calling him "Mr Gao", and still greets me loudly every time he is drunk, which is always.

Every day uncovered a new secret. When my landlady dropped by announced at 8am (as Chinese landladies do) for a chat, she told me about her childhood farming wheat in the district of Beijing that is now 798 art zone. I raised an eyebrow to discover she was a Red Guard in her teens, and had persecuted landlords in struggle sessions. She hung wooden signs over the landlords' necks denouncing them as capitalists, and made them take the "airplane" position – body bent forwards from the waist at a right angle, arms held out straight behind – for hours. "The changes really are big," I mentioned, "now you're the landlady." But she was bewildered. "I'm not a landlady," she said. "I just collect your rent."

For months I was haunted by Peking Opera singing that drifted faintly through one of my walls, stirring arias floating between construction drilling. On the morning of Christmas Eve, with fresh snow on the ground, I bumped into my neighbor Uncle Shi as he was taking out the trash in his pajamas. I asked who the mysterious singer was. He looked at me obliquely, then broke into a piercing rendition of "You And Me", the Beijing Olympics theme song, followed by "Silent Night" in beautiful, butchered English ("Alll is carrrm! alll is blight!"). Uncle Shi moved out some months later, the Russian couple moved in, and the Peking Opera arias were replaced by high squealing of another sort.

I'll never forget the midwinter night when, winding home through the *hutong* labyrinth, I came across a small bonfire on the street. Two young women were feeding it with cardboard, and had chalked a circle around the open flame. I didn't know about ghost day customs, and felt it would be intrusive to ask. When I turned the corner there was another flame, then another, and again, and charred dead fires besides them and an old man striking matches into the wind. I thought of them as cat's eyes guiding me home. Eventually I stopped a young man as he put fake paper money into his fire, and asked him why. "For the departed loved ones," he said. His father had passed away when he was small. I walked the last twenty yards home, and switched on all the lights.

It didn't take long before the changes outpaced new discoveries. The cheap family restaurant that I loved transformed itself overnight into a Korean stir-fry joint, inexplicably serving each meal with a complementary bag of Twinings tea, which I also loved. A Japanese manga figurine store opened for business, and a cosplay shop opposite it, where I walked in on a group of teenagers dressed up as comic book heroines. An imported wine boutique, run by the rather clueless Mr Liu from Shandong, opened and closed within months. Even the neighborhood sex toy shop was converted into a flat. Only the hair salons and the migrant brothels seemed to be in no danger of losing demand.

Two other establishments that never change a brick are the mahjong parlor – curtained and shuttered like a front for the mob – and the local showers, from which emerge the fleshy slaps and pops of massage and fire cupping. Opposite them is another watering hole, this one for local foreigners (we embrace the oxymoron). Cuju bar, named for the ancient Chinese sport that is almost but not entirely unlike football, is a sports bar, rum bar and Moroccan bistro all squeezed into one, a cocktail of influences we owe to its owner Badr. Some early mornings, while Mrs Wang is out buying her groceries, Americans cram inside to watch March Madness or the World Series. I saw my first Super Bowl there purely by accident, when I was going out to buy eggs for breakfast.

But the two worlds never seem to overlap. Expats drink Negronis and vape on the porch of Cuju, while older Chinese residents chug Tsingtaos and suck on Eights on the corner opposite. Sometimes the rival gangs eye each other, as if they are about to break into a West Side Story moment – the *laowai* and the *laotou*. There is a tangible suspicion about the influx of foreigners; the mahjong parlor installed surveillance cameras outside the week after Cuju opened. At least in those early days, I felt in the stares of my neighbors the assumption that we were outsiders passing through, as transient as the shops which opened and closed every month.

Mr Xi has been turning his home into a fortress ever since I moved in, although I keep telling myself there's no connection. First he erected a steel gate outside his front door. Then he railed off the back-door staircase, to stop others from locking their bikes to it. Finally, in the spring, he broadened his horizons by adding an extra story (perhaps he was a fan of Tang poetry). His neighbors learnt of his decision when a construction team started laying bricks on the roof, until his building was exactly a half meter taller than my own, and conveniently blocked the once lovely scenery over the rooftops from my study window where I did most of my writing. I dubbed it the ugliest view in the world.

One morning, two very fierce looking *chengguan*, the urban management police, showed up. They told Mr Xi that his impromptu addition was illegal, and another team of workers tore through its roof with pneumatic drills. Then they just left it there, for Mr Xi to take the rest down. Mrs Wang gossiped to me later that one of our neighbors must have called the *chengguan* as the building was blocking their sunlight. To this day no one knows who it was. Mr Xi left the building as it was – roofless, unpainted, loose bricks lying on top of the walls directly over the entrance – for over a year. I had half a mind to call up the *chengguan* to mention this, but remembered Kaiser Kuo's mantra for foreigners in China, "don't be a whiny little bitch".

While Mr Xi kept the neighbors out, I finally felt settled in. As spring turned to summer I planted vegetables on my rooftop, and failed miserably: the pak choi was decimated by bugs, the tomatoes were scorched by the sun, the aubergines and courgettes never made it out of the seed. Some mornings I did tai chi up there too, swiveling around to see hundreds of gawking faces pressed up against the school classroom windows. I could negotiate the labyrinth now, and became friends with our local *kuaidi* delivery guy. It had taken over a year, but my neighbors were finally greeting me back by name, stopping for a chat rather than simply looking at me.

I suspect it was the dog. James and Christina, an author and a journalist, had moved into the flat below me (we called our building "writers' block") and Christina found a stray dog on the street, flea-ridden and pitiful. They already had two dogs, Calvin and Hobbes, and I was now living alone, so they so deposited Ginger upstairs with me despite my protestations that I was a cat person. Within a month I had formally adopted Ginger, and entered a hitherto closed society of dog owners, who exchanged curt nods while our pets sniffed each other's rear in a canine yin yang. To the community, I was no longer a foreigner. I was a foreigner with a dog, which meant neither of us would be leaving anytime soon.

Between Ginger's constitutionals and a new habit of jogging before sunset, I got to know a wider radius around me. Each run excavated a fresh finding. The perpetually pajama-clad Mr E, whose retirement project was to endlessly decorate his tuk-tuk with colorful stars, stuffed animals and two flags on a weekly rotation. The fish store owner who painted classical landscapes. The old codger who I thought was chirping at me until he produced a cricket from his inside jacket pocket. The hunchbacked lady who beat her dog with a badminton racket (and is possibly a lovely person otherwise, if not likely so). When jogging through one block of *hutongs* got old, I moved on to explore the next one across.

I counted the passing months by yellow hutong weasel sightings. The critters only came out in the dead of night or pre-dawn hours, flashing past like a gunshot, and I might see two or three a year. If they were the true long-term residents, the *hutongs* were shifting around them. By weasel number five, the stir-fry and Twinings restaurant had become a fruit stall. At weasel number six, the manga figurine store was an electric scooter shop, and Miss Muesli, a homemade granola store, had opened opposite. The cosplay hangout became a bistro café around the time of weasel sighting seven. Sometimes one would get up on its hind paws and look about for a second, as if to warn us: Nanluoguxiang is coming.

The foreigners came and went too, although that was as true of the young Chinese who lived in the courtyard. The Russians had split up, and the sounds of loud Slavic coitus were replaced by Maxim's band rehearsing "Stand By Me" and "Don't Worry Be Happy". James hosted a weekly roleplaying game downstairs, and I spectated while the group talked and rolled dice for half an hour before realizing that in the fictional realm of Rokugan only five seconds of action had passed. When one new arrival in Beijing asked me about the floating *liuxu* fluff balls in spring, the willow catkin pollen, I told him it was PM 2.5. Every leaving party for an expat friend felt like our own ghost day ritual – burning paper money for the departed.

My neighbor Christina wrote an article about how the very aspects of *hutong* life that draw foreigners to live here put off Chinese looking for more modern conveniences. "The same old downtown area," she wrote of our district, "has become a hotspot for hipster expats ... who ride bikes, watch earnest documentaries, do tai chi on our rooftops." Burn. But for better or worse, when your breakfast options include doughy *youtiao* from the street market and custom-made granola from a shop called Miss Muesli, it's clear that the neighborhood has evolved to accommodate its foreign population, and isn't going to change back.

A year after the roof of Mr Xi's extra story was knocked down by the *chengguan*, he evidently figured that enough time had past, hired a new team to reroof and tar it over, and fixed his solar power cylinders on the top. He kitted out the rooftop next to it with wooden furniture, dangled vines from metal beams, grew watermelon, and put in a chicken coop. By now I was used to it, and he was used to me. He gave me the combination code to his fortress so I could lock my bike inside, and his ten-year-old son waves at me when he climbs the steps outside my study window.

Foreigners in China have always tried to romanticize the place. My go-to example is Karl Eskelund, a Danish journalist here in the 1930s (he later became famous for punching Chiang Kai-Shek's son) who wrote: "Peking has no tooting motorcars, no smoky factories, no ugly modern concrete buildings. The temples, the mysterious Forbidden City, the cozy dwelling houses with their intricate courtyards and gracefully slanting roofs, all stand today as they did when Peking was capital of the Middle Kingdom." Perhaps it's that projection of an authentic past that we idealize – until we're swept along by the authentic present, with its tooting motorcars and ugly modern concrete buildings, which is far more interesting.

When it comes to the *hutongs*, I don't get what's romantic about gray painted alleyways speckled with dog poo and spit. But they do force you to be part of a neighborhood, and to change along with it. When the present becomes the past at such rapid clip as it does in China, you can find yourself feeling nostalgic for something from only a year ago, as if it was ten years gone. Yet it's that sense of community and premature nostalgia that creates the esprit de corps, and keeps those who have left coming back.

I have friends who can stake a much better claim to their *hutong* than I – who have pigeon aviaries on their roof, or a blocked-off escape tunnel in their basement. Tom Pellman, my co-editor on this anthology, has lived in Ju'er Hutong, one block west of me, for six years. It's the same *hutong* Peter Hessler lived in and wrote about (we're both fanboys), and long before him Edmund Backhouse wasn't far away (ditto). Between VPN clampdowns and visa worries, on a bad China day it can feel like we're not welcome here. The government's narrative after the century of humiliation seems to be that foreigners might pass through China, but will never belong. Yet everyone is swept along in the same flux. We make our own homes, and take them with us.

Ten years on, perhaps the lanky Englishman will be just another memory for Mrs Wang. I like to think she'll still be here, rooting through a box of pak choi in the veggie market at the entrance while a new generation of foreigners pass by. Much of Xiguan Hutong will no doubt be different, but the kernel will be the same – a constant defined by cycles of change. And some days, in the brief hiatus between summer and winter, when the first cold bites and it feels like the year has reset, there's even a beauty to the haze of smog that disperses light evenly over the narrow alley walls and all the life squeezed in between them. In moments like that, I can't imagine being anywhere else.

IF NOT FOR THE MELON

Flash fiction

Daniel Tam-Claiborne

WE DISCUSSED IT, and after a time decided on the watermelon. What if the landlord doesn't drink, we wondered, or if he hates sweets. Watermelon was neutral, we reasoned; something we could all agree on.

My roommate bought it on her way home, one of those massive ones you see stacked in the back of a minivan idling by the side of the road. She took it on the bus to the landlord's house herself – up front in the priority seats, her arms wrapped around the watermelon on her lap like she was three weeks from bursting.

The landlord wasn't obligated to invite us over for dinner, but he said he wanted to. He couldn't remember when he started doing it, but he had been renting out the apartment in Beijing for decades and it was just something he liked to do.

When he came to the door, he was wearing a baggy t-shirt draped over a pair of gray sweatpants, like he had just woken up from a nap. "We brought you this," my roommate said, gesturing to her midsection. He laughed a little when he saw it, as if gifting a watermelon revealed something innate about her character.

"I'm sorry my house is such a mess," the landlord said. It wasn't dirty so much as cluttered. We took off our shoes and said nothing about the boxes draped in table linens stacked floor-to-ceiling against every wall of the apartment.

We sat down and started drinking tea. When we finished, the landlord poured us each a measure of *baijiu* into the same glass. The watermelon sat between us in the center of the table, like an interloper, the characters in the name itself signifying its foreignness. *Xigua*, western melon.

"To friendship," the landlord said, before tossing his head back and emptying the glass. We drank ours down too, the clear alcohol slowly corroding the backs of our throats. "One more?" he asked, holding the bottle out in front of us. But we both waved our hands, no, in front of our faces, albeit a bit too quickly.

The landlord withdrew to the kitchen. "Most of the food is already prepared, he said, I just need to heat it up." In all, he had made six dishes: cabbage and mushroom, pickled cucumber, potatoes and cauliflower, stir-fried egg and tomato, pork ribs, beef seared in an iron skillet. He smiled when our eyes perked up: "I wanted to make sure you ate well."

It was only when we could barely stand the sight of the still half-full plates that the landlord abruptly spoke out. "The melon!" It was sitting in plain sight for so long that we nearly forgot it was there. He came back from the kitchen brandishing a cleaver big enough to use as a movie prop and sliced off a large chunk for each of us. How funny, I thought, that this once foreign object no longer felt the least bit out of place.

The watermelon was juicy and sweet and perfect for a summer night. Before I arrived, I had never thought twice about spitting out my seeds, but in China I adopted the convention of poking them through with the end of a chopstick. It was common practice, but it still felt entirely novel to me. How funny, I thought, that this once foreign object no longer felt the least bit out of place.

"When you go back to America," the landlord said. "You will miss food like we have here. Everything will be different."

He wiped his mouth with the back of his hand. I looked down, tracing the shimmery liquid in the bottom of my bowl, newly studded with black seeds.

Yes, I thought, though I wished it weren't true. But there will always be watermelon.

CONTRIBUTORS

Alec Ash ("In the Hutong") is a writer and journalist in Beijing, founder and non-fiction editor of the Anthill. His book about young China, *Wish Lanterns*, is forthcoming from Picador.

Cobus Block ("Life is an Internet Café") lived in China from 2008 to 2010, was a Fulbright scholar in Kazakhstan, and now lives in his home state of Nebraska, where he works in international business development.

Brent Crane ("Ramadan in Kashgar") is an American journalist and writer currently based in Cambodia.

Sam Duncan ("Ayi and I") spent four years in China, studying Chinese and then working as an English teacher. He is now based in Seoul.

Tom Fearon ("State of Media") is a former copy editor at CCTV News and Global Times, and has lived in China since 2009.

Jesse Field ("Awkward Lavender") lives in Beijing, where he teaches literature at Peking University Associated High School.

Aaron Fox-Lerner ("Back and Forth") was born in Los Angeles and lives in Beijing. His writing has appeared in the *Los Angeles Review of Books*, *Bound Off* and elsewhere.

Courtney Han ("Roots and Leaves") left Beijing at the age of five but remains a resident in spirit. She is now based in Boston, where she writes fiction and studies international development.

Robert Foyle Hunwick ("Shower Business") is a writer and editor in Beijing. He is working on a book about vice, crime and China's other attractions for I.B. Tauris.

Jeremiah Jenne ("The Mountain Spirits are Laughing") is a rogue sinologist and writer from New Hampshire living in Beijing.

Karoline Kan ("Examining the Past") is from Tianjin, and works in Beijing as a journalist at Radio France Internationale.

Jonathan Kos-Read ("I'm Not a Communist, But I Play One on TV") is an American film and television actor, well-known in China by his stage name Cao Cao.

Kaiser Kuo ("Old Chokey Christmas") combines China hand and metal head, is co-host of the Sinica podcast and works at Baidu, which has been described as "like Jon Bon Jovi went to Google".

Mia Li ("Over the Wall") lives in Beijing, where she is a researcher for *The New York Times* by day. At night, she turns that news into stand-up comedy.

Hannah Lincoln ("Love, Anywhere") lives in Beijing and works in market research, while nursing a lifelong love for literature.

Alicia Lui ("Censor") lived in Beijing, where she co-captained Big Brother, an Ultimate Frisbee team. She now studies at University College London.

Tom Mangione ("Rice Fields") is a writer and musician living in Shanghai. He's a founder of the bilingual poetry group United Verses. When on stage, he goes by the name Ho-Tom the Conqueror.

Sascha Matuszak ("Flower Town") is a writer currently based out of Minneapolis. His stories have appeared in *The Economist, South China Morning Post, VICE* and *Roads and Kingdoms*.

Laszlo Montgomery ("Made in China") worked in Chinese manufacturing for twenty five years. He is now based in LA, and is the elusive genius behind the China History Podcast, available on iTunes.

Canaan Morse ("Nursery Rhyme for Beijing") is a literary translator formerly based in Beijing, now living in his homeland of Maine.

David Moser ("The Book of Changes") is Academic Director at CET Chinese Studies at Beijing Capital Normal University. He also plays jazz piano with various jazz groups in Beijing.

Magdalena Navarro ("Short Nails, White Socks") left Barcelona for Beijing five years ago but she still wants ice in her water.

Carlos Ottery ("Big in Beijing") lived in China from 2008 to 2014, and now hangs his hat in Cambodia.

Tom Pellman ("The Tiger Suit") lives in Beijing and is fiction editor of the Anthill.

Jonathan Rechtman ("Model Worker") is a Chinese-English simultaneous interpreter based in Beijing, specializing in international conferences and bar mitzvahs.

Peta Zhimin Rush ("Family Footsteps") was born in Singapore and grew up in the UK. She is currently studying Chinese and teaching English at Sichuan University in Chengdu.

Michael Salmon ("Dumplings") was born in London but has been living in Dalian for a while.

Carl Setzer ("The Cornfield Grave") is originally from Ohio, and has lived in China for over eleven years. With his wife Liu Fang he runs Great Leap Brewing, a craft brewery in Beijing.

Rosalyn Shih ("Mid-Autumn Lanterns") is from Hong Kong and lives in Beijing, where she co-runs the Beijing Contact Improvisation group.

Josh Stenberg ("The View") is an Asia-based writer whose work has appeared in various journals and anthologies. He has translated two volumes of Su Tong's fiction and edited *Irina's Hat: New Short Stories from China*.

Daniel Tam-Claiborne ("If Not for the Melon") is a writer formerly based in Beijing, where he worked as a Gruber Fellow in Global Justice and Women's Rights at the China Foundation for Poverty Alleviation.

Anthony Tao ("Writers in China") lives in Beijing, where he edits the blog Beijing Cream and coordinates the Bookworm Literary Festival. His poetry has appeared in various journals.

Yuan Yang ("Emei City") was born in Emei, Sichuan, and moved to the UK when she was six. She lives in London, where she writes about economics, and also poetry.

NOTES

"The Tiger Suit" was read aloud at the Anthill's Scotch & Stories night at the Beijing Bookworm, on May 27th 2015.

"Big in Beijing" was read aloud at the Anthill's Writers & Rum night at Cuju bar, on April 16th 2014.

"Back and Forth" was first published in the Beijing e-zine *Concrete Flux* as "Migrant with the Machine Gun Arm".

"Old Chokey Christmas" first appeared on the back page of *The Beijinger* as "In Winter".

"Love, Anywhere" is also anthologised in Hannah Lincoln's collection of her stories, *Ashen*.

"If Not for the Melon" won the 2014 Beijing Cream Flash Fiction Competition, held at Great Leap Brewing. "Censor" was a runner up.